"Lynn Guerin listened very carefully to my  with Dad to learn, to understand, and to c life lessons, and coaching expertise. He disciple of Dad's Pyramid of Success and has worked enthusiastically and tirelessly to apply it to his own life and prepare to teach it to others. This book will help you understand what made my Dad such a remarkable coach and teacher and an even better person. It will help you coach yourself and provide momentum for your journey to be your very best. Dad would be so pleased to know his teaching is still making a difference at a time when his life lessons are more important and more needed than ever."

—JIM WOODEN, SON OF COACH JOHN WOODEN

"I had the honor and privilege to have played for Coach and, as a member of his last championship team at UCLA in 1975, the good fortune to learn each and every day directly from him. Like many of my teammates and the players before us, at the time we didn't fully appreciate or understand it, but Coach's life lessons were going to have a very positive impact on our lives.

"Through the ups and downs of my professional career, I always tried to stay true to Coach's success behaviors including Integrity, Honesty, Loyalty, Team Spirit, and Industriousness (Hard Work), which are some of my favorites. It wasn't, however, until I had the opportunity to work for Starbucks Coffee Company that I truly was able to apply what is described in the book as the Wooden Coaching Model and the Five Lessons for Leading. It all started with me, and there was not a day that I did not strive to model Coach's success behaviors. As a leader within the Starbucks Store Development Organization my teams were known for doing things the 'right way' no matter what the challenges and while always striving to be the best we were capable of being, we were able to accomplish some incredible things. I have no doubt that my success as a leader was a direct result of my commitment to live life The John Wooden Way. With *Coach 'Em Way Up*, Lynn and Jason have created the perfect tool to introduce you or expand your knowledge of Coach's behavior and leadership philosophies."

—JIM SPILLANE, FORMER SVP U.S. STORE DEVELOPMENT, STARBUCKS COFFEE COMPANY AND UCLA BASKETBALL TEAM MEMBER, 1973–1977, NCAA CHAMPIONS 1975

Coach 'Em Way Up

FIVE LESSONS

For Leading The John Wooden Way

LYNN GUERIN & JASON LAVIN WITH JIM EBER

Entrepreneur Press®

Entrepreneur Press, Publisher
Cover Design: Andrew Welyczko
Production and Composition: Eliot House Productions

This publication is designed to provide accurate and authoritative information
in regard to the subject matter covered. It is sold with the understanding that the
publisher is not engaged in rendering legal, accounting, or other professional services.
If legal advice or other expert assistance is required, the services of a competent
professional person should be sought.

John Wooden photo: Michael Gordon/Shutterstock.com

An application to register this book for cataloging has been submitted to the Library
of Congress.

ISBN 978-1-64201-121-0 (paperback) | ISBN 978-1-61308-442-7 (ebook)

Printed in the United States of America

25 24 23 22 21   10 9 8 7 6 5 4 3 2 1

To Coach Wooden, his family, and
the current and next generation of coaches

Contents

PART I

The Wooden Coaching Model

PART II

Five Lessons for Leading

Answering the Call to Greatness and Goodness

Foreword

by Sam Reese, CEO of Vistage

As the CEO of Vistage, I am blessed with the opportunity to work with nearly 25,000 CEOs and business owners across the globe as they pursue their paths to becoming better leaders, making better decisions, and driving better results. On my very first day leading the company in 2016, I noticed John Wooden's Pyramid of Success and its framework for achieving Competitive Greatness on the walls of the offices of many members of my executive team. Just like my days as a young athlete in Wheatridge, Colorado, I knew Coach Wooden's principles would help guide me once again.

Like most athletes growing up in the 1970's, the success of Coach Wooden was a reference point for every coach I encountered. The success of his UCLA basketball teams with legends such as Kareem Abdul-Jabbar, Bill Walton, and (my favorite) Keith Wilkes had me and countless high-school boys and girls nationwide dreaming of college basketball stardom. Even if we did not understand the depth of his lessons and our coaches lacked the patience of Coach Wooden, we were captivated by his concepts of team-work, effort, unselfishness, and integrity.

I eventually found my success on the track, not the hardwood. I was recruited by colleges nationwide after winning two team and two individual state titles before my senior year in high school, and I used Coach Wooden's Pyramid of Success principles of self-control, conditioning, and confidence to drive me. After an injury early in my senior season, several colleges lost interest in me, but the University of Colorado still offered me a scholarship. Without that offer, I would not have been able to attend college, let alone pursue my dream of becoming an Olympian.

I posted some of the best cross-country times in the country as a sophomore at Colorado and became a first team All-American in 1982. I signed my first shoe sponsorship deal with Nike that same year. It would be the last year I ran competitively. A series of injuries and subsequent surgeries forever ended my Olympic dream. After graduating from college, I headed towards a traditional career path, which felt like a disappointment. I longed for something that felt as important and motivating as my track and field career. I was lost and only found what I was looking for after I was promoted into my first management position and felt the generous weight of leadership responsibility.

To guide me, I once again turned to John Wooden and his Pyramid of Success to help me build the character and confidence of the teams I managed. At the same time, the Pyramid guided me and reminded me of how far I still needed to go to fulfill my potential as a leader. That is even truer for me today at Vistage.

Vistage is one of the world's largest CEO membership organizations. I had benefitted so much personally from the insights and coaching I had received as a Vistage member for fifteen years while I was running a successful training company. The Vistage model is anchored around a peer advisory structure led by a Vistage Chair (i.e., coach) who brings together local CEOs to help each other work on their most challenging issues and opportunities. When I took the job as Vistage's CEO, I knew it would be an incredible adventure *and* an incredible challenge to lead a company with more than 1,000 chairs and nearly 25,000 members. Add to that the fact that the Chairs and members are experienced CEOs, and it can be daunting to think you bring added value to the equation. I had to raise my leadership game immensely. But seeing those Pyramids on the walls around Vistage inspired me and reminded me how far I had come as a leader and how I still needed to set the example for those I was leading and serving. The leadership lessons of Coach Wooden tightly align with our purpose of helping high integrity leaders make great decisions that benefit their companies, families and communities.

Today, I have a front-row seat watching thousands of CEOs focus on their own leadership potential, and I have found that those who embrace John Wooden's principles are the ones who see sustained success and balance. Like me, they know the Pyramid of Success and its framework for achieving Competitive Greatness. We admire it and the man who created it. We truly understand the importance of being consistent in our behavior and in our personal and professional lives. Just like Coach Wooden, we know that self-improvement is a never-ending challenge. We are more energized by the challenge to improve than by pushing toward a crowning achievement. And we know that by teaching and mentoring others we turbocharge our own engines and continue to get better and better.

But while so many of us know the Pyramid of Success, we have never had a tool that expanded upon and codified what the Pyramid and John Wooden's approach to leadership could do for us today—a book that laid out a practical approach for integrating them into our lives and organizations. Until now. Thanks to Lynn Guerin and Jason Lavin (a long-time member of Vistage) the lessons from this book will undoubtedly help keep us all committed to improvement and remind us of the possibilities we see in ourselves and in each other.

Finding Coach and the "Wooden Way"

Why John Wooden?

Google "50 greatest coaches of all time," and you'll see a lot of debate on who is number two. Most lists have one name at the top: John Wooden. But who is John Wooden, and why do we need him today? What does a man who coached his last game in 1975 and passed away in 2010 have to say to leaders and coaches today about how to coach yourself, your team, and your business up—all the way up? Turns out, more than either of us ever imagined. John Wooden transformed the way we think, lead, and coach, as you will hear in our stories, told in the first person in the first two chapters. What will he mean to your story as you prepare to improve your thinking, leading, and coaching the Wooden Way?

*"The best competition
I have is against myself to
become better."*

CHAPTER 1

Employment Means Nothing: Jason's Story

I graduated USC in 1992 and continued my career in service. Specifically, I was a waiter. My parents begged me to look for an office job. "Maybe you will like it," they said. But I knew how to serve. I liked doing it. I believed I could own the Good Earth restaurant franchise I worked in one day. That would be something for a middle-class kid from Tustin, California, who put himself through college working there 40 hours a week (and with student loans). Nevertheless, I honored my parents' wishes and looked for something else. With no family connections or business network, that meant first scanning the help wanted section, which was futile. Then I thought about the customers I waited on and remembered Floyd.

I had waited on Floyd Wicks and his family for years. He came in every Sunday with his wife and kid. Other servers would run when they arrived. They're so picky. Not me. I wanted them at my table. Chamomile tea with ice on the side; orange juice, no pulp; and hot chocolate but not too hot. It was the same thing every time.

Picky perhaps but easy to execute and make them feel taken care of the moment they arrived.

Floyd always said to "look him up" at the water company he worked at when I was done with college. Did he mean it? I decided to ask the next time they came into the restaurant.

"Mr. Wicks, remember when you told me that when I was done with school I should look you up?"

Before he could answer, his wife grabbed him and said, "Hire him!"

Floyd told me to send him my resume. My resume said, "graduated college and managed and waited tables at the Good Earth restaurant." Not even a professional resume writer could do much with those credentials. My friend Jerry, who had already succeeded in getting a corporate job after graduation, suggested that I should at least know something about the company and what Floyd did there before sending anything, so I called the water company and asked for some corporate literature. When Floyd said he worked at the Southern California Water Company, I thought that meant he replaced plastic jugs in office water dispensers. Nope. According to the information I received, the Southern California Water Company was listed on the New York Stock Exchange, employed hundreds of people, and served hundreds of thousands of customers. At the front of the annual report was a letter from Floyd E. Wicks, CEO.

Floyd hired me despite my feather-light resume, and they put me in the MIS, or Management Information Systems department, because they figured a recent college grad had to know something about computers. But I had never used a computer, let alone afford one. I didn't understand any of it. WordPerfect? Lotus 1–2–3? DOS . . . what's a DOS? MIS was understandably less than thrilled to have me and my lack of experience. I was only there because I was "Floyd's Guy."

My manager, Bob, was less than enthusiastic to have me on board, accepted that I was his new project, and told me that work started the next day at 9 A.M. sharp. I showed up at 8:45 and reported to my desk and computer. With nothing valuable to do, I was told to delete all the files the previous person left behind. That was all I did my first day and pretty much my first two weeks. Delete. Delete. Delete. When people would walk by my desk, I would lean in toward the monitor, pretending to be working on something important. At the end of those two weeks, Floyd's secretary, Georgette, called me out while I ate lunch in the cafeteria.

"You have been given a huge opportunity. The very least you could do is show up on time," she said.

"What? I come in 15 minutes early every day."

"Don't lie to me," she beady-eyed me. "I've seen you walk in late every day."

She told me work started at 8:30 A.M., not 9, and the look on my face told her I had no idea and had been the victim of some hazing. She demanded I tell her who told me to come in at 9, and I did. They reprimanded Bob (and eventually fired him). Everybody loved Bob. Now everybody really loved me (not). I was Floyd's Guy. I didn't like what I was doing. I can barely turn on a computer and do anything but delete files. And I got Bob in trouble. I was so miserable I went back to the MIS department and went on a delete binge until the day ended. Delete. Delete. Delete. Delete. Delete. Delete. Delete. Delete. Delete.

The next day I came in at 8:15 and my computer wouldn't turn on. I asked for help from the only guy who didn't resent me, and he couldn't figure it out, either. Then he realized someone had deleted DOS. He looked at me: "It's getting bad around here. Bob got busted, and now someone sabotaged your computer."

He didn't know it was all me being completely ignorant and that I was the one who deleted my entire operating system. I was useless. I went to see Floyd to give him my two-week's notice. He asked why. I told him the whole story. "I don't have anything to do. I don't have any skills. I got Bob in trouble. I ruined a computer. I need to go back to the restaurant. That's where I belong."

"Before you quit, I need you to make me one promise."

"Sure, Floyd, anything."

"I need you to write a paper for me on how we can train every employee here to treat people like you treated my family at the restaurant."

"That would be valuable to you?"

"Very. Do that for me, and then you can quit."

I never finished the paper, but I never quit, either. Before I could complete my assignment, Floyd hired Diane Rentfrow, a retired Air

Force officer, as his manager of employee development. Floyd told her about my paper. Diane looked at what I had started, and with her help, the company's first customer service training module was born. I could do customer service, I thought. I'd learned the art of it at the restaurant. I won customers like Floyd over with customer service principles, and he'd overheard me training the other waiters and staff. Now Floyd and Diane were sending me to Shipley Associates' Customer Service Training (which later was acquired by and became part of FranklinCovey) in Salt Lake City, Utah. When I returned, I started adapting what I learned to our industry, and with Diane leading the charge and with unconditional support from Floyd as CEO, we wrote the company's first customer service training curriculum. I presented it to the executives at the first class with Diane and then proceeded to put everyone in the company through it.

Teaching customer service at a water utility company in the 1990s was unheard of. There were no water companies anywhere doing customer service training with this level of executive commitment. There was no need. Back then, like today, most water companies were owned by municipalities. The rest, like Southern California Water Company, were private (i.e., investor-owned). But we all shared one thing: a lack of competition. Residents had no choice in who delivered their water. They still don't, though today customers have the internet and social media to post reviews and launch campaigns against those companies with poor service.

All that didn't matter to Floyd. He saw our "competitors" as department stores and banks and restaurants—anyone and any company that delivered a service. He wanted our service to be the equal of the best anywhere (as good as it was at the Good Earth when I served him), and he put Diane in charge of it with me by her side. I was promoted from intern to employee development generalist, and with the full support of the CEO's office, we didn't just help create that training program, we built Southern California Water Company University. We modeled the curriculum after other corporate programs like Disney University and Motorola University, and next to water quality, nothing was more important than the employee development linked to the education and training programs we ran. The university was so successful at motivating employees, boosting morale, and increasing integrity and competence (in addition to providing great service), Diane rebranded it as "Employee Development University," with the idea of selling its training programs to other water companies that were beginning to understand Floyd's way of thinking. Teaching them was no threat to us. After all, they were not our competitors. The goal was to make the university pay for itself or even become a profit center for Southern California Water Company.

I watched and learned as I helped Diane execute everything involving the university and all employee training, and she became not only my boss but my mentor. She taught me lessons I have carried with me to this day, like "Employment means nothing. Be employable." Employment can be taken from you at any time. You can do a great job and still lose your job. Employability can never be taken from you. She wanted to make me employable, because when you're employable, you know you can leave at any time and get another job. She drove this point home one morning when she found me, like most mornings before work started, reading the sports section. I played baseball when I was a teenager and had a giant collection of baseball cards. I was obsessed with reading the back of baseball cards as a kid, and it carried over to combing the baseball box scores as an adult. Diane asked how that was working out for me. I told her it was working out great. Here we are together, in Figure 1–1 on page 10 .

"So, how's your career in baseball turning out?" she asked. "Jason, what are you thinking about all day? I would suggest you swap those box scores for this." She handed me *The Wall Street Journal*. "I want you to read this in the morning because your future is in business, not baseball. If you want to be successful, you're going to have to change how you're thinking."

Diane's words were life changing for me. From that moment on, how I was thinking became synonymous with the business acumen I demanded of myself and everyone who worked for me since then. That meant doing things like reading books and watching business and news media, staying up-to-date on trends, contributing new ideas, understanding the big picture, exhibiting curiosity—all things I was not doing when I read the sports section in the office.

FIGURE 1–1 *Jason and his first mentor, Diane Rentfrow, in 1997*

▲ ▼ ▲

I worked with Diane for eight years at Southern California Water Company. For five of those years, I drove her to and from work. Diane hated to drive, and our relationship became a kind of *Driving Miss Daisy* situation. We became quite close. Four days per week I would drive her home after work, and she and her husband, Bill, would feed me dinner, and afterward Bill taught me computer stuff. Before long, I started to master the things I was clueless about when I was working in MIS.

While I worked at Southern California Water Company with Diane during the day, I built my first website with Bill's help at night.

My friend Jerry, who worked at an advertising agency, had asked me if I knew anyone who could do a website. I thought for a moment. "No, but I can do it."

"No, man . . . I'm being serious. This is for one of our clients. I need to find someone who can build a website."

"I don't know anyone, sorry. I still think I can do it, though."

We hung up. A couple weeks went by, and Jerry called back, "Do you really think you can build a website?"

"Yes, I can do it!"

"OK, what do you need from us?"

"I need $5,000. And I need half of it up front."

Jerry's company sent me a check for $2,500.

I used that money to buy my first computer (a Gateway 486). I finished that website for Jerry's client, Atlantis Submarines, and then built a site for another customer and another and another. I got so good at building sites that people paid me even more for my work, and from those nights in Diane and Bill's house, my company GoldenComm was born.

But GoldenComm stayed a side hustle for me, especially after I had a chance encounter at Diedrich Coffee Shop in Costa Mesa. A woman in front of me had ordered a coffee drink with nine nouns and adjectives, and I smiled and asked her if she was going to "put Wild Turkey in it too, because it already sounded terrible." She laughed and said, "Do you have a job?" She introduced herself: Cynthia Nelson, a recruiter in the booming field of cellular communications. She was working for growing companies that needed to hire talented people. Business was booming, and she had a gut feeling about me. I didn't even know what a recruiter was, but within an hour of our conversation, she told me she could get me a job that paid $20,000 more than I was making to do new employee development, training, and orientation at L.A. Cellular. I couldn't say no.

Within a year, I was like the mayor of the company; I knew and served everyone. Either I trained them on their first day, or I worked with their managers and trained them on customer service. My enthusiasm rubbed off on people, and I loved the work, particularly making sure new people had a great first day. Even as I was promoted, I insisted on keeping that "first day" job. Others before me hated that part of the job, but to me the first impression was the most important one. The difficulty was in the eye of the beholder, just like serving Floyd and his family in the restaurant.

L.A. Cellular was acquired by AT&T in 1999, and my job only got bigger as the market expanded. In the early 2000s, opportunity was everywhere in wireless communications, and it wasn't long before AT&T wanted me to relocate to Redmond, Washington. I turned them down. I was getting married and needed to stay in Southern California. I wasn't sure what would happen next when Dan, a sales manager who was in one of my first-day orientation classes, asked me to come work for the sales division and "double my salary." They wanted me to be in the "advanced services organization" and sell wireless data to police, fire, and other first responders. All my computer and internet training with Bill and Diane was paying off big time for me. Because of my computer knowledge, I was the only salesperson who did not need an engineer with me on sales calls. I stayed at AT&T Wireless for a couple more years but soon got recruited by Sierra Wireless at a trade show and doubled my salary again, selling wireless technology to companies like Cisco, Intel, and Amazon (for a product they were launching called Kindle). I was 32 years old, traveling the world to visit some of the biggest companies in the world, and already making more money than I ever thought I would.

And then there was GoldenComm. The market for websites had been growing too, and the business had become much more than a side hustle: Ten employees and a growing roster of clients with me, the owner, spending his days selling for another company. By 2007, it became untenable to do both, plus my wife, Brenda, and I just had our third child. I had to choose: my $300,000 per year job, plus stock options and benefits, or run GoldenComm. It wasn't a question of money for me but risk. A lot of people call me an entrepreneur, and I always object. If I were an entrepreneur, I already would have been running GoldenComm for years. What I was and am is a risk mitigator, and for me, working at my own company was a high-risk proposition—all the risk and none of the security of working for someone else. But I also knew I had succeeded in everything I had done by outworking everyone else. I had a feeling I could do that if

I went all in at GoldenComm. I became my company's 11th employee. What's the worst thing that could happen? I thought. I was about to find out.

Things were going great at GoldenComm until the crash of 2008. Sixty-five percent of our revenue came from mortgage companies, and by the start of 2009, almost all of them had closed their doors. GoldenComm started burning cash, first the company's then mine. I started dipping into the second mortgage on my house, and we held on. Then my bank reneged on my home equity line of credit, and I lost access to the little cash I had.

I asked my wife, "Do you realize how badly I messed this up?" I had everything and now I had nothing. We and our kids were about to be homeless because I couldn't pay our mortgage again. I went to HUD to see if I could save our house. I was a wreck when I told all this to Andrew, one of my first employees.

"We can't make payroll. All our clients are gone. I'm at the end."

"JL, I have some money."

"Andrew, I appreciate that, but this is a bigger problem than it probably looks. . . . How much have you got?"

"About $200,000."

"You have $200,000?"

"JL, I'm Vietnamese. I save everything. I'll give it to you."

"I might never be able to pay you back."

"Oh, you will. We can do this."

I took it.

We made it.

▲ ▼ ▲

By early 2010, we were back on track, making our clients' websites work harder. I spent millions of dollars developing our own techniques, systems, and ecommerce and content management platforms. Everything was proprietary to us. We called it the GoldenComm Lead Machine (GCLM for short). I thought it was a great product. So did our clients. And it was. It worked for them and my company. It just didn't work for my team. No one cared about the GCLM except the 50 people who worked on it. The result? I kept losing employees. Because while our product was working, my people weren't growing. They couldn't leverage their work for us into bigger jobs in technology and broaden our standing in the industry. Putting "GoldenComm Lead Machine" on a resume meant nothing to anyone but us, so their stock went down.

Our Lead Machine also made GoldenComm an island. The world of technology was and is a very collaborative place. My people couldn't connect with others in the community who used mainstream platforms to solve problems and source ideas, because no one understood what we did. This made the stock of my people who understood our code go way up inside the company. They were our demigods. If they were unavailable and people ran into a problem? Everything was on hold until they got back.

It took longer than I care to admit, but I finally remembered what Diane taught me about employment versus employability. My people were not employable the way their peers were. The person who tipped me in that direction was my business partner in Pune, India, Ankur Agarwal, the CEO of Clarion Technologies and one of the brightest people I have met in the world. During one of my trips to India to visit Ankur, he suggested we mainstream the programming side of GoldenComm and the GCLM. That was it. I did what Diane told me. I changed my thinking. We left the GCLM behind and joined the mainstream. Things changed quickly for the better. Developers stayed longer because they felt like what they were doing was more applicable outside our company, and they were contributing to their profession and their personal growth. The clients didn't notice a thing. If anything, we solved things faster for them.

In the wake of all this change, I began to think about the overall culture of GoldenComm. I believe a great culture is why people want to work for a company. That culture should be defined by a clear leadership philosophy and a shared set of values. We taught and trained around five values at GoldenComm: learn, change, grow, do, and serve. I thought they were good values, but of course I did. They were mine. The values of the company were just like the Lead Machine: "Jason's Way."

Why in the heck am I in charge of the philosophies and the behaviors of this company? Who am I? I'm nobody except to these 70 people.

If I owed it to my people to mainstream the proprietary part of our products, then I owed them a voice in thinking about and owning the values we would work and live by. I wanted to get away from "Jason's Way" to a way we all could align around to help us move forward. We needed a new set of values, and we needed a coach to help us get there—to help coach me, them, and us through the process together.

We looked at lots of people and resources to guide us through the process of developing a leadership framework and methodology that focused on behavioral not operational change to help us and GoldenComm be our best. But we didn't want some "flavor of the month" to lead us. We wanted something tried and true. Dale Carnegie, Napoleon Hill, Stephen Covey . . . those were the resources I gravitated to, as did the team. We needed someone who valued resources like those as well. In fact, we had mostly settled on a certified FranklinCovey facilitator when I decided to do one last "treasure hunt" and look at the search results beyond page one for leadership trainers and consultants. GoldenComm was now number one in search engine optimization (SEO) around the world, so I knew how easy it was to miss good options online. Page one captures most search traffic clicks. If a company—even a great company—didn't understand the importance of SEO, they would be on pages two, three, and four. On page three, something caught my attention: The John R. Wooden Course.

As a sports fan, I knew a bit about John Wooden's legendary coaching career at UCLA (even if, as a USC grad, I didn't take too kindly to the results): Between 1964 and 1975, his UCLA men's basketball teams had four undefeated seasons and won 38 straight NCAA Basketball Tournament games, seven championships in a row, and ten championships overall—the tenth coming in the final game he coached. All are records likely never to be broken. But I knew little about John Wooden's story and never studied his framework for achieving competitive greatness—The Pyramid of Success—and I liked what read about them and the course based on them. The course, like the Pyramid, was behavior-driven, not operationally driven. John Wooden led his teams to competitive greatness (results) by following his Pyramid's 25 behaviors and characteristics (see Figure 1–2 on page 16). They were the foundation for the way he lived his life and treated others, and he needed just 28 awesome words in plain English to

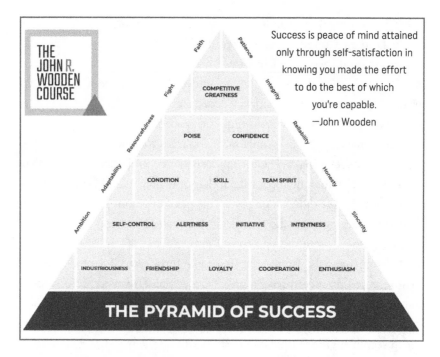

FIGURE 1–2 *The Pyramid of Success*

spell out what those behaviors and characteristics were. (Only three blocks had more than one word.) The course would take our team through all of them and make the Pyramid our framework for success as it was for Coach Wooden. It all felt to me, in a word, "timeless."

The John R. Wooden Course had a name to contact for more information, Lynn Guerin, and a local 714 area code. I dialed the number. Lynn answered the phone.

"My name is Jason Lavin. I have a problem. I have a company of around 70 people, mostly millennials, and most of them have never heard of John Wooden or The Pyramid of Success."

"We should change that," Lynn said.

"I agree."

▲ ▼ ▲

Lynn came over to GoldenComm and presented The Pyramid of Success to me and how he works with companies. He had a "Coaching Success

Course Series" that he had developed with John Wooden before he died on foundations and fundamentals, the Pyramid, how to be a head coach, and developing extraordinary teams. He also had an online assessment that could evaluate the team against all 25 blocks of the Pyramid. I loved the assessment. I loved the curriculum. I didn't love the giant three-ring curriculum binders that Lynn brought with him for the team. If I presented those binders to my millennial team and told them to use them, they would look at me like I told them to start using a rotary telephone. I told Lynn just to talk to them the way he talked to me about Coach Wooden and the Pyramid. I knew they would respond. They did. We were all in.

I hired Lynn and we set a date for an off-site with my leadership team. By the end of the day we met with Lynn and heard more about the Pyramid and course, all of us knew this was it. We were going to insert the Pyramid into our company. And we did—in so many ways, including making it the writing on the wall: We placed 25 signs featuring each block of the Pyramid around the office along with quotes from John Wooden and other great coaches as a reminder to live them every day.

What I didn't know at the time was my work with Lynn would not only transform our culture at GoldenComm, but that I would never think about the way my company executed its business the same way again. We would rework our peer review evaluation system using the Pyramid. We would change our hiring practices to include the Pyramid. We would even use blocks from the Pyramid to do lessons learned post-projects. And that was just about the work. I would never think about success, coaching, or my story the same way again. My search inside—to coach myself and my team way up—was about to begin with Lynn and lessons from the greatest coach who ever lived.

*"Everyone in their life
must have someone and
something to which they are
loyal if they are to have
true peace within."*

CHAPTER 2

It's All About Coaching: Lynn's Story

I met John Wooden in the spring of 1996. He was 86 years old and had not coached a basketball game in 21 years. But he had been staying busy shepherding the Wooden family, speaking, writing poetry and books, and providing counsel to organizations, coaches, and leaders. Just doing the things legends do when the phone seldom stops ringing with calls from people seeking an audience or some wisdom and guidance.

I was one of those people, but I had no idea John Wooden would become *the* role model for me as a teacher, coach, father, grandfather, husband, and mentor.

▲ ▼ ▲

As a young athlete growing up in the 1960s in northern Ohio, I was very aware of college basketball but not John Wooden's West Coast version. My hometown hero, Larry Siegfried, was a star guard with future NBA Hall of Famers Jerry Lucas and John Havlicek on the 1960 Ohio State team that won the national championship. John Wooden, then in his 12th season at UCLA, had not yet won his first

NCAA Championship, and was in the midst of a 14–12 season—the worst he would have in his 27 years there. Meanwhile, I was trying to find a way to make my mark in a football-crazy small town, earn a college athletic scholarship, and get past being poor and a third-generation abandoned son. Fathers in my family had walked away from their boys for over a hundred years. My dad left when I was three. The task of raising me, my two brothers, and my sister fell to my loving, hardworking mom, her mother, and a series of stepdads.

By the time John Wooden started his run of championships, I had overcome a life-threatening industrial accident that almost cost me my right leg, dropping out of high school to preserve my senior season of eligibility, and come back to be part of an undefeated championship football team. I earned all-state honors and a college scholarship to Western Michigan University and became the first in the Guerin family to go to and graduate college. I earned a bachelor's degree in liberal arts with a minor in Black-American studies and then a master's degree in cross cultural international studies. This was a time of social and racial unrest in the United States. I had experienced economic prejudice, but having grown up in an all-white town, I was trying to figure out life as it was playing out in places like Detroit. I interviewed with Detroit congressman John Conyers to be an assistant but did not get the job. I had worked summers at Pontiac Motors and National Motor Castings, but I thought I would like to teach and coach instead, perhaps in social studies in the city. I ended up taking a more traditional path, taking a sales job at an industrial division of Johnson & Johnson.

At Johnson & Johnson, I had the "corporate leadership" look that was expected for men in my position—three-piece suit, wing-tip shoes, crisp shirts with cufflinks, and a striking tie—and expectations for a predictable 20-year climb up the corporate and social ladder. Work my way into management. Become a vice president. Have a secretary. Get married. Get those stock options. Buy a big house. *I can do this—I can be what the title on my business card says I am,* I thought.

My definition of success was the dictionary definition: the accumulation of material possessions and or the attainment of a position of power and prestige. At this point, I knew no other definition.

Five years with Johnson & Johnson was followed by a stint with General Electric, managing marketing, communications, events, and training and learning leadership behavior and models of success from men like Jack Welch. Welch was brilliant, demanding, intense, and often intimidating. His game was hockey growing up, and he played the game of business much the same way: fast and tough. Control the ice, protect your goal, and deliver the blow—what the scoreboard reads when the horn sounds is all that matters. Few at GE were brave enough to challenge Welch on the strategy or the details of their businesses. Everyone wanted to please him. Failure was not an option. In fact, we lived in fear of failure. You had to be good, or you were likely to be gone, part of the bottom 10 to 20 percent Welch famously eliminated every year.

It was at GE that I first felt something was missing for me in this corporate approach to business and culture, but I couldn't articulate what it was.

My next move up the corporate ladder and into the heady world of consulting, corporate training, and performance improvement was at the Sandy Corporation. Sandy's mission was to "close the gap between potential and performance" for large organizations, especially for automotive companies, and help them do big things. We worked with General Motors to launch new car and truck models every year, training thousands of people to sell, service, and support its nationwide dealer network. We reorganized, repurposed, and redesigned nearly $3 billion of educational programming for IBM into a "systems approach to education," improving focus, delivery, and consistency and accelerating performance levels. We launched Infiniti as a Japanese luxury brand from the ground up, establishing standards and procedures for every phase of the customers' total-owner experience; training every employee nationwide in a unique eight-day training academy; and turning them into 150 high-performing teams.

Much like I did at Johnson & Johnson and GE, I learned important business lessons at Sandy I would never forget from those programs and especially speeches delivered by the company's founder and world-class phrase turner, William Sandy. But again, something was missing for me. All our work was about revenue creation and success in the short run. There had to be a bigger definition of success out there somewhere.

My first opportunity to find that definition would be to strike out on my own. My Sandy experience had taken me from Troy, Michigan, to Irvine, California, and I decided to leave corporate America and launch my own company, Guerin Marketing Services. I had more than enough experience and contacts and confidence in selling and executing performance-improvement projects to believe I could be successful, at least by that dictionary definition, at running my own business. Two years later, we won a competitive bid to launch the University of Toyota and create a curriculum, management development process, and tools for its corporate managers and nationwide dealer network.

Toyota had a reputation for seeking the best American minds, such as W. Edwards Deming and his 14 Points for Total Quality Management in the 1950s. For its university, delivering the Total Quality Experience became an important goal and "coaching" a key idea to help managers create the kind of teamwork that would produce that Total Quality Experience at the dealerships. To understand what great coaching was and meant, we decided to reach out to some of the best American coaches ever, bring them in, put them on camera, and interview them about their coaching philosophy, processes, methods, and approaches.

We wanted to create courses to teach people how to win. In the automotive world that meant "moving the metal"—making those ten-day sales reports look good, keeping the service team busy, and keeping the bosses happy. But Toyota as a company was also process driven when it came to quality. The Toyota Production System had raised the industry bar with its continual analysis, attention to detail, and continuous-improvement approach to building the highest-quality products. I felt if we could find that same high-quality approach when it came to people, building teams, and providing inspired leadership in our work with the coaches we brought in, we could create a more enlightened view of success.

Enter John Wooden.

▲ ▼ ▲

It made good sense to start with the man ESPN would later call the "Coach of the Century." No one had achieved the results John Wooden had, but as we quickly discovered, he was about much more than results and coaching basketball. He knew what inspired leadership looked like. He not only led great teams that could perform at extraordinary levels over extended periods of time but had defined success differently than any dictionary. To him, success was "peace of mind attained only through self-satisfaction in knowing you made the effort to do the best of which you are capable." This was the definition I had been looking for, and it was backed by something much bigger: his Pyramid of Success.

The Pyramid of Success was as complete a blueprint as I had ever seen of critical behaviors needed to achieve success as John Wooden defined it. It was perfect for creating a consistent language of behavior, expectations for team members and actions by management, and a team culture in which excellence was the standard and perfection always the goal—and more than just a possibility as Coach Wooden's four undefeated UCLA teams could attest. At the pinnacle of the Pyramid was what every team and business is ultimately after: competitive greatness. Reaching competitive greatness required using the foundations and fundamentals of the other 24 behaviors and characteristics that surround and support it. It required *preparation*, *effort*, and *enthusiasm*. It came through being *disciplined*, *alert*, *conditioned*, and *skilled*. By putting the *team* first. By maintaining *poise* and showing *confidence*. By exercising *patience* and always having *faith*. Those were only some of the words that appeared on his Pyramid.

What word did not appear? *Winning.*

Of course winning was one of the outcomes of competitive greatness, and John Wooden's teams won a lot. His college teams posted a total record of 664–162 and his UCLA teams went a remarkable 345–22 during the 12 years they won those ten national championships. But unlike many of the leaders I worked with in corporate America, Wooden never talked about winning (or losing) and certainly never entertained the idea of "winning at all costs." He believed in teaching others to win by setting a standard higher than winning. To him, there was no greater joy than living a life and being involved in work that benefitted other people. Sharing and giving of yourself was exercising the credo that "it is more blessed to give than to receive." He understood helping others meant not expecting anything in return. He helped people because it was the right thing to do, and he was always willing to give of his time. He followed the Golden Rule ("do unto others as you would have them do unto you") and expected those he served to follow.

Simply put, John Wooden wanted to make all of us better *humans*. As legendary broadcaster Dick Enberg said, John Wooden's "greatness [was] only exceeded by his goodness"—the greatness he demanded of himself and others and the goodness he shared with everyone he coached and met. This greatness and goodness of John Wooden—his wisdom, insights, and life lessons; business and leadership principles; coaching methods; and Pyramid of Success not only provided the Toyota solution we needed but, to me, held out great promise for something much bigger: a more complete way to coach, counsel, and help others; a better model for a business in developing people and organizations to be their best; and maybe—just maybe—a path to create a much better version of myself.

In hindsight, one moment during the Toyota University initiative stands out to me as the beginning of what I wanted that version of me to be and the role the man I now called "Coach" might play. Coach was not actively involved in the creation of the curriculum, but we filmed Q&As with him at Toyota's USA headquarters to use within the curriculum's modules. We had just wrapped one of those recording sessions with the project team when I was handed a note that said very senior Toyota executives from Japan were in town. They had heard the "legendary John Wooden" was on site and asked if he would be available to join them for lunch in the executive dining room. He said he would be honored. We assembled at a single, large round table, but Coach was still clearly at the "head" and the center of attention. There were brief introductions, a little small talk, and a short question and answer before the salad arrived and there was a lull in the conversation. That's when Coach politely asked the mostly Shinto and Buddhist executives if he could offer a blessing and say grace, as was his custom at every meal. They were happy to abide. He bowed his head and said a short prayer of thanksgiving and blessing for God's favor, protection, direction, and guidance.

A simple prayer, a definable difference, a lasting lesson for every person at the table and something that strengthens my faith to this day. He demonstrated to me in that moment that you should never be ashamed of who you are, what you believe, and what you have been taught. He was living the Pyramid as he had for more than half a century, showing poise in action by being true to himself.

The deeper I dove into all things John Wooden, the more I became personally impacted and convinced we could do bigger things together. Coach had a technique for keeping your attention. To help you listen more attentively, he would speak a little slower and a little softer. I would have to move a little closer to hear him. Moving closer to John Wooden was always a great thing. Being around and with Coach made you want to be a better person in every aspect of your life. And I wanted more of that—and him. I had never encountered such fundamentally sound, powerful, valuable, and inspiring ideas on how an individual, a team, or an organization could become their best and be successful. I believed anyone, not just me, could benefit from the example Coach set as a person and a professional. Anyone could learn to coach themselves and others to be their best to improve their lives and the world they lived in if they spent each day on The Pyramid of Success. Every business could build strong teams and a culture of consideration, cooperation, collaboration, and excellence.

The entrepreneur in me was excited as my big idea became crystal clear in my mind: The John R. Wooden Course. It could be done in a way that had lasting impact, meaning, and purpose. I would work with Coach to capture his wisdom, experience, philosophy, methods, processes, and content in a way that had not been done before in any of his books: So it could be *taught* to leaders and teams in businesses, schools, and even families to make them stronger. To make us all better humans.

I decided to write my idea up a five-page letter to Coach suggesting a partnership between the two of us (or rather, Guerin Marketing Services and the Wooden Family Trust). I scheduled an appointment with Coach at his Encino home and spent three hours discussing the possibilities, answering questions, and considering some important details. Finally, it was time for a decision.

He said no.

▲ ▼ ▲

Coach was incredibly kind in turning me down. He liked the idea and very much appreciated my industriousness and enthusiasm in pulling the idea together. But it was late in the fourth quarter of his life. He wasn't sure how long he would be available as a business partner. He said he should have done something like the course 20 years earlier.

I had learned in working with Coach that his "yes" was yes and his "no" meant no. But when he said no, I didn't hear it. I thought of one of the words at the top of his Pyramid: fight. Competitive greatness did not come from giving up. Coach had also referenced the cornerstones of the Pyramid—industriousness and enthusiasm—in his rejection of my idea. I knew there was much more work to be done in addition to the course. I suggested we keep working together on projects like Toyota. Maybe we could revisit the idea in the process. I had already identified another opportunity with Nissan USA. He said he was enjoying working together, so let's keep doing that and maybe we could revisit the idea for the course.

It took a year, but Coach finally changed his mind. It was a senior executive conference we designed for 300 Nissan managers in Las Vegas that turned him around. A Nissan client of mine said his sales and service managers nationwide were divided into eight regions, and each was doing its own thing in its own way. "They're all wearing different colored jerseys," he said. "I want them 'playing' like they're all on the same team." So in the morning session, we had Coach teach and inspire them on what a championship team looks, sounds, acts, and performs like—how they treat each other and work together. We built a 20-foot Pyramid of Success for the stage and put all the managers in the same colored shirt, or "jersey," to hear Coach speak.

In a morning session, Coach noticed that three managers in the audience had failed to put on that jersey. He shifted his presentation and shared some of his team's rules on proper dress: If you're out of proper uniform, you don't travel, practice, or play. Repeated violations would mean you lose your privilege to be part of the team. His message was heard. All three people returned from morning break with their jerseys on.

After that conference, Coach revisited the idea of the course and changed his mind. I worked directly with him to design, develop, and write the curriculum and launch strategy. The Wooden family designated Craig Impelman to represent them and coordinated with Coach to tell his stories, which was invaluable to me. Craig was married to Coach's granddaughter

Christy and had been around Coach at both UCLA and the family dinner table, always listening and learning. He was a basketball coach himself and had a gift for teaching children basketball skills and inspiring adults with Coach's wisdom and life principles. He ran John Wooden basketball camps and taught a management seminar based on a few of Coach's principles. He even helped build his own successful business, a credit-collection agency, using The Pyramid of Success behaviors. Today, he also designs and writes the "Wooden's Wisdom" coaching newsletter. The only one who knew more than Craig about all things Coach, on and off the court, was of course Coach. Here we are together in Figure 2–1.

Craig became an essential part of the course's construction, but it was my time with Coach that was transformative for me and the curriculum. We wrote 160 pages of content based on the answers to questions about how his life became his life. His values. The way he grew up. The way he defined success and created his Pyramid. How he used it to get results yet surround himself and those around him with love and balance. Everything I heard impacted me personally and caused me to think about what I was

doing and how I was getting it done. Every day working with Wooden, his wisdom kept flowing and my questions kept coming.

Was my head on straight? Coach was always referring to the quality of your thinking: What you think determines what you do and ultimately who you become. When he talked about his father Joshua's advice to "drink deeply from good books, especially the Bible," he wasn't preaching. He was saying that today we get too much bad information, in too many ways, too quickly. What comes out of your mouth and actions and life will only be as good as what goes into your head. If we let it into our minds, it will soon be into our heart, soul, and everyday behavior.

Was I setting a good example? First for my sons and family, then for the people I worked with and for. Were my actions speaking louder than my words? Was I doing the right things for the right reasons? Was I kind, consistent, fair, and considerate in the way I was treating people? Or did I have my "what's-in-it-for-me?" hat on?

Was I the same guy when everybody was looking that I was when no one was looking? His answers provided direction every day, not just in how I wanted to pull our course together but in how I wanted to pull my own life together.

With Coach on my shoulder, I was working hard to get every aspect of my life on a track that would enable me to finish strong, just the way he was. Refiring not retiring and making the rest of my days the best of my days for my family and for anybody else that I might have an opportunity to teach, coach, and serve.

▲ ▼ ▲

Coach died in 2010 at the age of 99, but we continued to refine and evolve his course after he passed, adding assessments and new lessons based on the Pyramid and the work we did while he was alive. While Coach's life and the Pyramid remain the core of the course and this book, the assessments and lessons as they apply to coaching yourself and your team in business and in life are unique. They became the foundation of the work I did with Jason and his team at GoldenComm—and continue to do with them as they have become our partners.

What Jason and I know and have come to understand on an even deeper level since finding Coach is the "Wooden Way" won't work unless you commit to coaching yourself first. Jason succeeded in meeting his people where they are because he knew where he was and where he'd been. You must use The Pyramid of Success and the lessons for leading that follow in the same way: Make them work for you and *then* your team to coach yourself and your team way up. That's what this book is all about:

- ▶ Developing your mindset, attitude, and skills as a coach
- ▶ Understanding and employing a complete blueprint for your behavior
- ▶ Developing habits that enable you to get the best out of yourself in the life that you live and the work that you do with and for others under the guidance of the greatest coach ever

Ready? Let the intersection of our stories serve as the foundation for you to discover Coach (maybe for the first time) and the great coach and leader who lives inside you. We will return to provide examples and coach you through this book. But for now, it's your turn to be working on it with us and Coach.

"There is no greater joy
than being involved
in something that
benefits others."

CHAPTER 3

Your Story

"Working on it." Those were among the final words spoken by John Wooden.

On his last day on Earth, with his family gathered around him, he asked his pastor to read from the gospel of Matthew: *Love the Lord your God with all your heart, with all your soul, and with all your strength.* This is the great and foremost commandment, and the second is similar: *Love your neighbor as yourself.*

When his pastor finished, he asked, "How did that go for you, Coach?"

"Still working on it," Coach replied.

"Which one are you working on right now?" his pastor asked.

"Loving God," Coach said.

Even in the final minutes of the fourth quarter of his life and with his final words, John Wooden was coaching himself and his family way up, showing the wisdom, faith, and love that was the hallmark of the way he lived and now defining the way he chose to complete his journey on Earth. Ever the teacher, he was working on the quality of his thinking and the values he lived by his entire adult life: respecting others, believing in God, seeking wisdom, doing the hard work, doing what's right, being positive, and never trying to be better than someone else—just being the best you can be.

This chapter starts the work of developing the coach inside of you in order to seize the opportunity to, accept the responsibility for, and understand the privilege of being the coach your people need you to be. It starts with a consideration of something Coach put a premium on for himself and everyone he coached: character.

CONSIDER CHARACTER

If Jim Collins showed us how to go from good to great, John Wooden showed us how to go from goodness to greatness—to care for others and build character and values that led to outstanding performance. Sure, the "scoreboard" was important to Coach; he knew the importance of winning to keep his or any job. If you are in management, you are responsible for delivering results, from hitting sales and profit objectives to fostering employee engagement and fueling innovation. If you are a teacher, your students must demonstrate growth and learning against certain benchmarks. If you are a coach of a team, you must win, which is what Coach did for 17 years before he won his first of ten championships. Not one of his college basketball teams ever had a losing record. But winning was not how Coach defined success and certainly not how he measured it, even after he won those championships. As Kareem Abdul-Jabbar, the NBA's all-time scoring leader and MVP of three of Coach's NCAA Championship teams, said in *The New York Times*, "Coach Wooden enjoyed winning, but he did not put winning above everything. He was more concerned that we became successful as human beings, that we earned our degrees, that we learned to make the right choices as adults and as parents."

Coach did what Kareem said by setting the example he wanted his team to follow. As the "Head Coach" of our teams and families, many of us have felt pressure to win at all costs *now* and to do things we know we should not; to make compromises we do not want to make—or know are inauthentic, and even wrong; and to consider others in the decisions we make. Coach never did this. He believed there was always a right way and a wrong way to do things, and the responsibility to do things the right way and *keep* doing them for himself, his team, and all the people he influenced and was responsible for started with *him*—no matter the circumstances. UCLA won all ten of its championships under Coach during some of the most turbulent times in American history. Yet despite what was going on in the world around him, he never failed to live by his Pyramid of Success, and he expected his team to follow suit. He had the ability to get the most out of a diverse group of people with disparate beliefs and come together around a shared set of values on the court (Coach's "workplace") and succeed as a team. And while he accepted his players would have differences and believe differently than him and each other, he did not suffer poor character. He placed strong character at the top of his list of desirable traits for his players, because no matter how or what they believed, players with strong character were:

- ▶ more considerate of and worked better with others;
- ▶ more giving and sharing-minded;
- ▶ more polite, courteous, and in tune with others; and
- ▶ more likely to use their ability to serve the team.

Is your team displaying this kind of character? *Are you?*

ALL THE WORK AHEAD STARTS WITH YOU

You are the constant in the Wooden Way to get the most out of yourself and the teams you will be privileged to work with. You will find certainty in uncertain times. Your teams may also be in a constant state of flux, just like Coach's were. Think about it: Few of the players John Wooden coached would be with him more than three years (freshmen were not allowed to play until 1972). Loyalty and fidelity to the team was expected but so was turnover—every year. New players, new competition, new challenges. . . . Coach knew competitive greatness was not something you achieved once and could rest. The work started over each season, building on and adjusting from the years before. That's how UCLA built a dynasty.

EXPECTATIONS OF CHARACTER

Coach never compromised on his expectations of character, even if it meant benching one of the best players in the history of UCLA: Sidney Wicks. In 1969, Wicks had his first chance to play as a sophomore, but he was selfish and would not play team basketball. Coach sat him until he got it. Wicks would say, "Coach, you know I'm better than anyone else on the team." Coach didn't disagree: "Yes, you are, Sidney. It's a shame they're beating you out, and the team isn't better with you." UCLA won the championship Wicks' sophomore year (Kareem Abdul-Jabbar's final season), with Wicks watching much of it from the bench. Wicks turned it around his final two seasons, and UCLA lost only three times with him as a starter, winning the championship both years.

Succeeding with an ever-changing team of people is a model for any leader today. You can't expect your best people to stay forever, either. You need the team you have to work together and succeed now *and* lay the foundation for future success. Many will likely move up or out. The one constant is *you*. You are the one who needs to keep working on the lessons.

Now it's time to start helping you understand the Wooden Way, assessing your own behavior and doing for you what John Wooden did for us and others, for more than half a century:

- ► guide you to achieve true success;
- ► prepare you to coach yourself and others to be the very best;
- ► challenge you to reach extraordinary levels of performance;
- ► motivate you to pursue not just greatness but also goodness; and
- ► inspire you to keep working on it!

This is your call to greatness and goodness in every phase of your life. Let's develop the mindset, the attitude, and the day-to-day behavior of a great coach in you. Let's start working on it!

THE WOODEN WAY WORKsheet

How Would Others Describe You?

John Wooden was often described as the "poet laureate of reason, kindness, and decency." If you were to survey your family, coworkers and employees, what three words would they use to describe you?

1. _____
2. _____
3. _____

If these three words become your legacy, would you be satisfied? If not, what three words would you choose that best describe how you want to be remembered?

1. _____
2. _____
3. _____

Now have the people whose opinion matters most to you perform this exercise with you, starting with your family. What three words did they use most?

1. _____
2. _____
3. _____

PART I

The Wooden Coaching Model

How am I executing now as a coach and leader?

Coach was far too humble to name anything after himself. As he wrote in his book *They Call Me Coach* (McGraw-Hill Education, 2003), "Talent is God-given; be humble. Fame is man-given; be thankful. Conceit is self-given; be careful." So, we did it for him. (Forgive us, Coach.) The Wooden Way is our name for your coaching game plan. It includes the Wooden Coaching Model, an Individual Assessment, and Five Leadership Lessons that work together to help you become the coach, not just the leader, you need to be.

The distinction between leader and coach was an essential one for John Wooden. He believed all great coaches were effective leaders, but not all effective leaders were great coaches. To him, a leader was a person who can get individuals to work together for the common good and the best possible results while at the same time letting them know they did it themselves. A coach was a thinker with a well-defined philosophy, a teacher who set the proper example, and a leader who was an industrious doer as well, commanding respect by his knowledge, hard-work ethic, and discipline. A coach was also a mentor who guided with wisdom, experience, and love.

To understand what this meant to Coach and start working on you, Part I of the Wooden Way focuses on:

- ▶ finding clarity in your own story—your foundations and fundamentals, your values, your way for defining and measuring success—through understanding Coach's story.

- ▶ assessing your own behavior with The Pyramid of Success to establish your current personal benchmark and guide future improvements.

- ▶ enhancing your understanding of each of the Pyramid's behaviors and using what you find to teach and coach yourself and others.

The goal of Part I is to find, define, test, and develop the coach in you (you will never coach anyone else any better than you coach yourself) and understand the importance of finding your own coach or coaches (*everybody* needs a coach) to guide you the way Coach guided Lynn and Lynn guided Jason.

"Success is peace of mind
attained only through
self-satisfaction in knowing
you made the effort to
do the best of which
you are capable."

CHAPTER 4

Your Foundations, Fundamentals, and Definition of Success

J ohn Wooden gave his best effort to finish strong, and no one finished stronger than he did on the court or in life. But how did it start? In this chapter, you'll read about the foundations and fundamentals that guided Coach's personal development, shaped his character, and produced his definition of success—and use them to write out and reflect on your own.

FOUNDATIONS AND FUNDAMENTALS

John Robert Wooden was born on a small farm in Hall, Indiana, in 1910, and, like so many Indiana boys, fell in love with basketball. For him, the love started when he was eight years old. His first hoop was an old tomato basket his father knocked the bottom out of and nailed in the hayloft of the barn. His first basketball was made of rags stuffed into his mother's old black cotton stockings, which she sewed by hand into as round a form as possible. "It's hard to imagine how, but I still think we were able to dribble that thing," Coach told Lynn.

Coach grew up with an overwhelming admiration for his father, Joshua. The philosophy of life that Coach developed (and the coach that he became) were largely the result of his father's love, guidance, and wisdom. His father was a man of few words and taught mostly by example through the level of effort he put into everything he did and the care and consideration he gave to everyone he met. But those few words had a huge impact on John, especially on the few occasions he wrote them down. For example, Joshua wrote down and gave John and his three brothers a very direct set of rules he called "Two Sets of Threes" to guide their everyday behavior.

The first set dealt with integrity and being honest:

► Never lie.
► Never cheat.
► Never steal.

The second set dealt with how to handle adversity and difficult situations:

► Don't whine.
► Don't complain.
► Don't make excuses.

That second set of three would be familiar to every player John Wooden coached. He had a daily expectation to see a positive attitude from every player and coach every day. Anything less would be counterproductive and cancerous to morale. He felt whining was particularly destructive as it took the spotlight off the "we" and onto the "me." Whining created a negative environment and severely damaged team culture, wasted time and energy, shifted your focus from solutions to problems, stalled momentum, and required additional effort to get back on the right track.

But the biggest impact Joshua Wooden had on young John came when he graduated from grade school. "Try to live your life after these things," he told John as he gave his son a $2 bill and a piece of paper on which he had put his words and wisdom. This time he wrote a "Seven Point Creed"— seven suggestions for living a meaningful life:

1. Be true to yourself.

2. Help others.
3. Make each day your masterpiece.
4. Drink deeply from good books, especially the Bible.
5. Make friendship a fine art.
6. Build a shelter against a rainy day.
7. Pray for guidance, and give thanks for your blessings every day.

Coach read his father's Seven Point Creed every day of his life. He carried the paper his father wrote it on in his wallet until the print faded so badly, he had to rewrite each word. That creed eventually shaped the seven foundations and fundamentals that guided Coach's day-to-day behavior as a person, teacher, and coach for the rest of his life:

1. Love of wisdom as the highest form of knowledge
2. Care and consideration as the rule for treatment of others
3. Fairness in everything with everyone
4. Loyalty to someone and something
5. Respect for authority
6. Strong sense of purity and propriety
7. Love and balance in all things

What are the foundations and fundamentals in your life? Most of us say we have a set of values that we use as guideposts to live our own lives, to guide our children, and to influence our associates. Use the following worksheet to clarify and understand your own foundational elements.

THE WOODEN WAY WORKsheet

Foundations and Fundamentals

Take a moment to define your core values—those simple rules aimed at how you conduct yourself in life—the foundation of your principles that shaped who you are and what you believe today. Do not think about your business, but you specifically.

THE WOODEN WAY WORKsheet

_____

_____

_____

How were they established? Who influenced their creation?

_____

_____

_____

How do those values match with the words you and others used to describe you at the end of Chapter 3? Where is there alignment, and what is missing?

_____

_____

_____

Now, take those values and start developing your own creed, one that you could put on a card and share with those you love like Coach's father did with him. Joshua's had seven points. Your creed may contain more, or fewer, elements.

_____

_____

_____

DEFINING SUCCESS

As Coach worked on living his life by his father's suggestion and defining those foundations and fundamentals in his life, he also learned to play basketball with something other than his mother's stuffed stockings. He became a three-time Indiana all-state guard and led his high school team to the state title in 1927. He went on to play at Purdue where he became the first three-time consensus All-American in history. After graduating in 1932, he played professionally for teams whose names are lost to history like the Indianapolis Kautskys of the National Basketball League (one of two leagues that eventually merged to become the NBA). But the start of his professional basketball career was only the third most significant thing that happened to John Wooden in the year after he graduated. The first was he married his high school sweetheart, Nellie. The second was he took a position teaching high school English in Dayton, Kentucky—a decision that would define the following 78 years of his life and become the first test of the values his father instilled in him.

Soon after he started teaching, Coach grew troubled by the amount of pressure parents placed on their children to "succeed." No matter how much he attempted to dissuade them, most parents considered anything below an A or a B a failure. Sports had already taught him that losing didn't mean he was a loser, and he refused to judge his students based on a grade or a winning percentage. He disagreed with the idea of grades being the sole determinant of success as much as he disagreed with success being measured by fortune or fame, power or prestige. But he lacked an alternate definition. So he started working on one.

He started by reflecting on his own education. He had once believed what the parents of his students believed. In high school, he had been given an essay assignment from one of his teachers: define success. His definition included getting an A in his teacher's class. He was joking (mostly), but his teacher offered a different opinion: Success would not come from any grade; it could only come from "peace of mind." Coach combined his school memory with two important pieces of wisdom from his father. The first was from the Seven Point Creed: *Be true to yourself.* The second was something his father said to him that influenced Coach's core values:

"Never try to be better than somebody else, but never cease trying to be the best you can be. One is under your control. The other isn't." Finally, Coach reflected on a refrain he once saw hanging on the wall of the barbershop while he waited for a haircut: "At God's footstool to confess/A poor soul knelt and bowed his head/'I failed,' he cried./The master said, 'Thou didst thy best. That is success.'"

In these memories, Coach found the words that created his definition of success:

- ▶ "Peace of mind" from his teacher in high school
- ▶ "Self-satisfaction" from his father telling him to be true to himself
- ▶ "Effort" from his father telling him to never cease being the best he could be
- ▶ "Capability" from the refrain and the master telling his student he did not fail by doing what he was capable of

In 1934, Coach brought these words together in his definition of true success: *Success is peace of mind attained only through self-satisfaction in knowing you made the effort to do the best of which you're capable.* It took Coach the better part of two years to come up with the definition of success that would top his Pyramid. Most leaders don't take nearly that long, if they take any time at all. Do you? Do you have a definition of success, and do your people know what it is? Is success a win on the scoreboard (i.e., transactional); financial viability and adding value to shareholders and investors; the traditional business definition ("profit and prosperity"); something more like Coach's definition around peace of mind, self-satisfaction, effort, and capability; or all of the above? If you don't know what success is, how can you be sure you are going in the right direction or will recognize it when you get there?

Use the worksheets on pages 51 and 55 to define success for you or hone your definition.

THE PYRAMID OF SUCCESS

As soon as Coach had his definition of success, he realized something was missing. It wasn't producing what he expected from his students or their parents, and thus he had an even greater task: How could he fully

THE WOODEN WAY WORKsheet

Defining Success

What is your definition of true success? Write it down. (If you don't have one, write your first draft below now.)

_____

_____

_____

Where did your definition of success come from? Has it changed over time? In what ways?

_____

_____

_____

How does John Wooden's definition of success compare to yours, and why?

_____

_____

_____

How does your definition of success manifest itself and play out in your business and life? What do your teams and business use? Is it different from yours?

_____

_____

_____

FIGURE 4–1 *John Wooden and his handwritten Pyramid of Success. Photo ©UCLA.*

describe what was necessary to produce the type of success he had defined, both individually and as a member of a team? He had returned to Indiana from Kentucky to teach English and coach the football, basketball, and baseball teams at South Bend Central High School. How could he teach his definition of success to those he taught and coached? Coach told Lynn that in pursuit of the answers, he came across something called the "ladder of achievement." He considered the design but ultimately rejected it for a model based on the last of the Seven Wonders of the Ancient World: the Great Pyramid of Giza.

Coach began working on his Pyramid of Success (the exact one Jason encountered in Chapter 1) in 1932. He completed it 14 years later during his first college coaching job at Indiana State University in 1946. In 1948, he accepted the job at UCLA, and the Pyramid became an indelible part of his identity there, culminating with ten NCAA championships in his final 12 years. A testament to its timeless power, the Pyramid, along with a bust of Coach, still marks the end of Wooden Way (not to be confused with ours): the entire east concourse of Pauley Pavilion at UCLA. Display cases filled with photos and memorabilia tell the story of Coach and his work at the school. In the middle of the concourse is a quote from Coach explaining how he created his Pyramid:

> *Each block in the Pyramid was selected with meticulous care and consideration over many years and after a variety of experiences in my life. Some of the blocks selected in the early years were discarded when I concluded they were less than essential. Other blocks were out in different positions within the structure as I learned more with time. The position of each block and the specific order or the tiers of blocks in the Pyramid have great importance, starting with the foundation and cornerstones and building up to the apex: your own personal success.*

Coach would be pleased to see the Pyramid on the walls of UCLA, Jason's offices, and anywhere else. He would be delighted the Pyramid was and is still used as a teaching tool on courts and fields and in corporations, classrooms, and homes across the globe. He had no desire to keep the Pyramid his secret recipe. In fact, throughout his life, he personally mailed as many as 1,500 Pyramids per year to players, coaches, leaders, and anyone who asked. He wanted it to help others become the best they could be and maximize their success and the success of those they led by creating connection, consistency, and engagement and uniting everyone around a defined set of behaviors and values. But the Pyramid does not

THE WISDOM OF WOODEN • THE WISDOM OF WOODEN • THE WISDOM OF WOODEN

TRUE SUCCESS

When it comes to understanding Coach's definition of true success, one name comes to mind more than any other: Swen Nater. The lanky Dutch teenager who was once an orphan did not start to develop as an athlete until Don Johnson, the basketball coach at Cypress College, discovered him. Johnson knew potential talent and unique physical capability when he saw it. He took Nater's 6-foot, 10-inch frame under his wing, and he turned Swen into a Community College All-American his sophomore year as well as an excellent student. Johnson had also been John Wooden's first All-American at UCLA, and when Nater's two years at Cypress were up, Johnson recommended him to Coach to continue his college career. But Coach already had Bill Walton, who would become a three-time national player of the year and one of the greatest college players of all time.

Where others might see an obstacle, Coach saw an opportunity. He thought Nater could be a success, just not in the way Johnson imagined. He felt Nater's size and tenacity would give Walton a tough workout in practice every day. Nater might never start a game, but he could contribute to making Walton and the team better. In the process, Nater would improve himself and possibly be ready for a professional basketball career in two years. Wooden offered Nater a scholarship and that role to play. Nater accepted both eagerly.

Nater understood Coach's definition of success, which sat atop his Pyramid. He had peace of mind and self-satisfaction. He put in the effort to do the best he was capable of. He stayed on the Pyramid and gave Walton, the best college player in the country, all he could handle. Together, the big men won two championships together. And Coach was right: Swen Nater never started a college game, but he was more than ready for the pros. He was a first-round ABA and NBA draft pick, a two-time NBA All-Star, and the only player in history to lead the ABA and NBA in rebounding. He and Coach remained close friends until the day Coach died.

THE WOODEN WAY WORKsheet

Measuring and Achieving Success

Coach had a Pyramid of Success that guided him. What is guiding you to achieve your definition of success?

_____

How you are measuring your success? What kind of "scoreboard" do you use?

_____

Are those measures based on what you earn and how much you own (salary; net worth; the value of your home, business, and things you have) or the quality of the relationships in your life (the value you bring to others, the joy in your family, the contribution to your community, and your desire to help, serve, and develop others)?

_____

What behaviors and characteristics do you value most and measure yourself against to achieve your definition of success?

_____

Take the time to align your answers above. What are three things you can do right now at the start of your success behavior game plan?

_____

_____

_____

work by osmosis. It is not enough to post it on the wall and hope everyone reads and follows it. It only works if the leader as head coach commits to modeling each of the behaviors every day. That requires buying into a higher view of success and asking the question: *How am I executing against this definition of success?* And that is what the assessment you will take next is all about.

Note: If you are interested in reading more about Coach's story and getting a deeper sense of him and his philosophy as a person, teacher, coach, and friend, read *Wooden: A Lifetime of Observation and Reflection On and Off the Court* (Contemporary Books), which Coach wrote in 1997 with his frequent coauthor, Steve Jamison. As you read, think about his perspectives and your favorite stories and how his thinking about his life makes you reflect on yours and where you might go next. Take time to write down the three most important ideas you learned from the book and how you can apply them in your work in *this* book.

*"The best way to
improve the team is
to improve myself."*

CHAPTER 5

Assessing Your Behavior with The Pyramid of Success

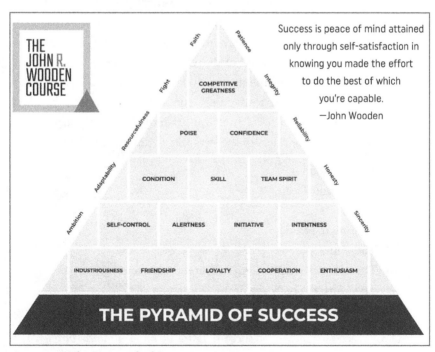

FIGURE 5–1 *The Pyramid of Success*

The idea for assessments for individuals and teams based on The Pyramid of Success came from Lynn's consulting and training experience with the Sandy Corporation, where developing solutions to solve client problems almost always started with a needs analysis of some type. He learned to ask the "classic" gap analysis questions:

▶ Where is the client's performance level now?
▶ Where does the client want its performance level to be?
▶ What is the gap between where they are and where they want to be?
▶ How can that gap between potential and performance be filled?

Lynn wanted to use the same approach in creating assessments for individuals, teams, and organizations to understand how their day-to-day behavior stacks up against The Pyramid of Success. The results would be to help those individuals, teams, and organizations figure out where they are and where they want and need to be when it comes to realizing their full potential. Coach Wooden thought the assessments were a good idea and the gap analysis logic sound, as he had spent his career as a teacher and coach working with basically the same idea. By 2004, the first assessments were ready, and In-N-Out Burger, a fast-food franchise legend in Southern California, became the first to put its 240 managers through a team assessment and training based on the results. The assessments continued to evolve from there.

The individual assessment that follows is designed to help you understand how your day-to-day behavior measures against each block and the Pyramid as a whole. It is broken into the seven parts, which correspond to the seven tiers of the Pyramid as Coach described them:

1. The Foundation
2. The Second Tier
3. The Heart
4. Nearing the Peak
5. The Pinnacle
6. The Mortar: The Strength of Human Character
7. The Mortar: The Force of the Human Spirit

These tiers build on each other from bottom to top and all working to achieve Coach's definition of success: *Peace of mind attained through self-satisfaction in knowing you made the effort to do the best of which you're capable.*

You will find a key for scoring each part at the end of the entire assessment. You can answer all 100 questions at once or go tier by tier, reflecting on each one as you proceed. To help you understand your answers, a description of each tier and all 25 blocks of the Pyramid follow in Chapter 6. Please, do not overthink your responses. There are no right and wrong answers, only your honest evaluation and an intentional opportunity to know yourself a little better.

TAKE THE ASSESSMENT ONLINE!

To save yourself the trouble of scoring the assessment yourself, you can pay a small fee to take it online at woodencourse.com. For readers of this book, we are offering the assessment for half price when you enter the code "Coach50" as the answer to the question: "How did you hear about the John R. Wooden Course?" The online version offers added value, including a detailed breakdown of your score, a Personal Pyramid Playbook, and exclusive videos for developing a 30-day action plan. We recommend using both the online assessment and the book in the chapters that follow as well as the lessons in Part II, which are exclusive to the book.

THE INDIVIDUAL ASSESSMENT

Please respond to each statement based on your current perception of your daily behavior using the following scale:

  0 = This statement never describes me and/or my behavior.
1–2 = This statement rarely describes me and/or my behavior.
3–4 = This statement describes me and/or my behavior a little less than half the time.
  5 = This statement describes me and/or my behavior half the time.
6–7 = This statement describes me and/or my behavior a little more than half the time.
8–9 = This statement describes me and/or my behavior almost all the time.
 10 = This statement describes me and/or my behavior all the time.

The Foundation	Your Score
1. I listen to the opinions of others before I offer my own opinion.	
2. Exercising proper judgment describes my approach to financial decisions.	
3. I am more interested in finding the best way than having my own way.	
4. I enjoy my job, and I am satisfied with my work experience.	
5. I work hard to get the job done right the first time.	
6. I have the respect of the people I work with.	
7. I weather difficult times and grow stronger from them.	
8. I enjoy being involved in a healthy exchange of ideas about the most effective way to accomplish important tasks.	
9. My enthusiasm as a leader encourages others to be their best.	
10. I enjoy hard work because I believe in the value of what I do.	
11. I develop my professional relationships into genuine friendships.	
12. I would not intentionally betray another person.	
13. I move forward with a clear sense of direction.	
14. My enthusiasm as a leader creates an atmosphere of encouragement.	
15. I work with diligence and consistency. I don't just go through the motions.	
16. I take the time to get to know others.	
17. You can tell from my life decisions that loyalty is one of my core values.	
18. I am cooperative when working with others.	
19. I do not whine or complain.	
20. I carefully plan my work.	

The Second Tier	Your Score
1. I maintain my composure during high-stress situations.	
2. My vision and mission are clear.	

COACH 'EM WAY UP

The Second Tier	Your Score
3. I have a vision and goals for my life.	
4. I learn from my mistakes and strive to improve.	
5. I maintain a positive attitude while serving others.	
6. I accept increasing amounts of responsibility.	
7. I am a patient person. I know good things take time.	
8. I am open-minded and adaptable, willing to take risks, fail, and grow.	
9. I accept personal accountability and monitor my behavior and performance.	
10. I am confident in my decision-making ability.	
11. I am not a quitter.	
12. I know of at least three ways I can improve.	
13. At work and at home I follow the rules.	
14. I communicate with confidence and compassion.	
15. Helping others be successful provides purpose in my life and work.	
16. I am aware of my strengths, and I am trying to improve my weaknesses.	

The Heart	Your Score
1. I take responsibility for developing the skills I need to perform my job to the best of my ability.	
2. "Team player" is an appropriate description for me.	
3. I am a highly competent person.	
4. I balance the hours I spend at work and home.	
5. I sacrifice personal aspirations for the good of the team.	
6. I feel prepared to handle every little detail of my job.	
7. I possess a healthy moral, mental, and physical condition.	
8. My attitude is positive.	
9. I perform the tasks of my work quickly and properly.	
10. I practice the fundamental aspects of my work to prepare for every challenge.	

The Heart	Your Score
11. I go out of my way to show appreciation for others.	
12. My job performance continues to improve.	

Nearing the Peak	Your Score
1. I learn from the leaders in my life and work.	
2. I am confident I can handle more responsibility.	
3. I feel composed and ready for any situation that may occur at my job.	
4. I am proud of the work I produce.	
5. I handle crises calmly and without panic.	
6. I do my best work under high-pressure situations when the deadline is drawing near.	
7. The only pressure I feel at work is the pressure I put on myself to do the best job I can.	
8. I am confident but not arrogant.	

The Pinnacle	Your Score
1. I believe things will work out for the best if I do the best I can.	
2. I enjoy tackling difficult issues at work because they challenge me to find creative solutions and perform at my highest levels of competency.	
3. I realize that not all things are under my control, so my circumstances do not define my attitude.	
4. I have faith that things will work out as they should, provided I do what I should.	
5. I have days that I would define as a "masterpiece."	
6. I take the time to make the best decisions.	
7. I am confident that things will turn out as they should.	
8. I am a great competitor and enjoy a difficult challenge.	
9. I am calm and patient when projects, tasks, or events take longer than I expect.	

The Pinnacle	Your Score
10. I make decisions that benefit others.	
11. I am more focused on doing and becoming my best than I am on winning.	
12. I realize it takes a long time to create excellence.	

The Mortar: The Strength of Human Character	Your Score
1. I do not intentionally mislead others.	
2. My communication style is direct and positive.	
3. I live my life in an ethical manner.	
4. I am reliable.	
5. I say what I mean and mean what I say.	
6. I am an authentic person.	
7. I never take credit for work I didn't perform.	
8. I ask for help when I am having difficulty completing a task.	
9. I am trustworthy.	
10. I am a sincere person.	
11. My behavior reflects the highest levels of integrity.	
12. I can depend on others to help me in difficult situations.	
13. I take responsibility for my mistakes and make the best effort to improve my performance.	
14. I act in a thoughtful and selfless way toward others.	
15. I admire the people I work with for the conviction of their beliefs.	
16. I trust other people who can impact my success.	

The Mortar: The Force of the Human Spirit	Your Score
1. I am ready to move when the opportunity arises.	
2. When I make mistakes, I recognize the error and work quickly to invent a solution to the problem at hand.	
3. No matter the situation, I find a way to do my best.	

The Mortar: The Force of the Human Spirit	Your Score
4. I am motivated to accomplish my work and goals.	
5. I do things quickly, but I don't hurry.	
6. I am flexible enough to meet the challenges created by changes in my life and work.	
7. I am a creative problem-solver.	
8. I discern between urgent and important matters because my priorities are clear.	
9. I stand my ground and remain true to what I believe is right.	
10. I have a healthy and proper respect for authority.	
11. I use the resources that I have been given.	
12. I refuse to compromise my ethical standards in my pursuit of success.	
13. I disagree without being disagreeable.	
14. I look for better ways to do things.	
15. I see challenging circumstances not as problems but as opportunities to test my abilities, learn, and grow.	
16. I am driven to achieve my goals.	

SCORING

Building up from the Pyramid's foundation, the assessment included four statements representing each of the 25 behaviors and characteristics of the Pyramid. Score yourself on each of the 25 behaviors and characteristics first, then total all your scores to grade yourself on the Pyramid overall.

Score Yourself on Each Block of the Pyramid

► Write your scores for each statement by its number in the grid below.

► Add your scores across each row. Write that number under TOTAL.

► Divide your TOTAL for each of the 25 blocks of the Pyramid by four. Write that number under SCORE. (Round to the nearest decimal. For example, round 8.75 to 8.8.)

The Foundation	Questions				Total	Score
Friendship	1	6	11	16		
Loyalty	2	7	12	17		
Cooperation	3	8	13	18		
Enthusiasm	4	9	14	19		
Industriousness	5	10	15	20		

The Second Tier	Questions				Total	Score
Self-Control	1	5	9	13		
Initiative	2	6	10	14		
Intentness	3	7	11	15		
Alertness	4	8	12	16		

The Heart	Questions				Total	Score
Condition	1	4	7	10		
Team Spirit	2	5	8	11		
Skill	3	6	9	12		

Nearing the Peak	Questions				Total	Score
Poise	1	3	5	7		
Confidence	2	4	6	8		

The Pinnacle	Questions				Total	Score
Faith	1	4	7	10		
Competitive Greatness	2	5	8	11		
Patience	3	6	9	12		

Mortar: The Strength of Human Character	Questions				Total	Score
Honesty	1	5	9	13		
Sincerity	2	6	10	14		
Integrity	3	7	11	15		
Reliability	4	8	12	16		

Mortar: The Force of the Human Spirit	Questions				Total	Score
Fight	1	5	9	13		
Adaptability	2	6	10	14		
Resourcefulness	3	7	11	15		
Ambition	4	8	12	16		

Score Yourself on the Pyramid Overall

▶ Add your TOTALS for all 25 blocks of the Pyramid and write that number under OVERALL TOTAL below.

▶ Divide your OVERALL TOTAL by 25 and write that number under OVERALL SCORE below. (Round to the nearest decimal. For example, round 8.75 to 8.8.)

Overall Total (Sum of All 25)	
Overall Score (Total/25)	

  0 = My behavior never aligns with The Pyramid of Success.

1–2 = My behavior rarely aligns with The Pyramid of Success.

3–4 = My behavior aligns with The Pyramid of Success a little less than half the time.

  5 = My behavior aligns with The Pyramid of Success half the time.

6–7 = My behavior aligns with The Pyramid of Success a little more than half the time.

8–9 = My behavior aligns with The Pyramid of Success almost all the time.

10 = My behavior aligns with The Pyramid of Success all the time.

Now that you have calculated your score, the next chapter operates as a worksheet for the assessment. It connects the statements to their corresponding blocks of the Pyramid, breaks down each tier and block on the Pyramid to understand its definition and what it means to you, then asks you to reflect on the assessment as a whole before starting the lessons on leading and coaching in Part II of The Wooden Way.

Remember: Coach didn't create his Pyramid of Success to build better basketball teams. He created it to help him be a better teacher and coach—to help himself so he could help others. He understood the power of asking yourself daily: *How am I doing?* Think of each block as a behavior and your "score" as how you are doing on that behavior right now. Then, make it a habit to improve on them. But know visible change will not happen right away. Think about the visible change you see when you exercise for a day or two—little to none. Stay with your efforts even if you don't see results after day one or even month one. Rid yourself of any behavior goals (i.e., improving your "score" on the Pyramid blocks) and fall in love with the behavior system (each block and the Pyramid itself). Work on the inputs, and the outputs will improve.

"It is what
you learn after you
know it all that
really counts."

CHAPTER 6

Understanding the Results of Your Assessment

The Pyramid of Success is a guide for getting you through the toughest of times, getting you ready for the best of times, and keeping you on track for being your best all the time. The assessment was designed to help you conduct a thorough, intentional, and honest self-evaluation using the Pyramid. Consider that as you look again at your scores and Coach's definitions of each block and tier of The Pyramid of Success that follow in this chapter. The definitions will broaden your understanding of each block and give you broader context for reflecting on your scores. We recommend having your scores from the assessment in front of you as you read.

HOW TO APPROACH THIS CHAPTER

A description of each tier and block of The Pyramid of Success follows. Each block follows this format:

- ▶ Name of the block.

- *Coach's definitions of that block in italics.* (The definitions evolved slightly over the years, including his work on the course with Lynn, but they mostly date to the original Pyramid.)
- The four statements from the assessment that correspond to that block of the Pyramid (in number order from that tier).
- Our descriptions of each tier and its blocks. (Some of the descriptions are self-explanatory and thus shorter than others, but all have their place and equal importance in the Pyramid.)

After the descriptions, you will see some lines. Use them to answer the following question, in addition to any other questions we ask before proceeding to the next block: *How am I doing—how do I demonstrate this behavior in my daily life and see myself as a coach and leader based on what I'm reading?*

THE FOUNDATION: THE CORNERSTONES OF INDUSTRIOUSNESS AND ENTHUSIASM

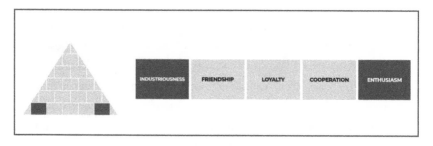

"No building is better than its structural foundation," Coach said, "and no man is better than his mental and moral foundation." While Coach didn't know how many blocks the Pyramid would have when he was done, he always knew that it had to have a solid foundation, starting with the cornerstones that hold everything together. Unlike many of the other blocks that changed their definitions and positions in the Pyramid's development, Coach knew what his cornerstones were from the beginning.

Industriousness

There is no substitute for work. Worthwhile results come from hard work and careful planning.

Industriousness Assessment Statements:

▶ 5. I work hard to get the job done right the first time.

▶ 10. I enjoy hard work because I believe in the value of what I do.

▶ 15. I work with diligence and consistency. I don't just go through the motions.

▶ 20. I carefully plan my work.

Without industriousness, you fail to develop the strengths that lie within you. Do you bring the necessary amount of effort when it counts? Coach demanded industriousness of himself and others in improving skills, building physical conditioning, and fine-tuning execution. But Coach also knew hard work without planning and direction was likely to be inefficient. He never took the easy way with his teams or relied on tricks or shortcuts. He often said, "Failure to prepare is preparing to fail," so his definition of industriousness always included planning, which is why two hours of careful planning went into every team practice. The process of and the discipline to plan is often where leaders and coaches see themselves falling short.

_____

_____

_____

_____

Enthusiasm

Enthusiasm brushes off on those with whom you come in contact. You must always truly enjoy what you are doing.

Enthusiasm Assessment Statements:

▶ 4. I enjoy my job, and I am satisfied with my work experience.

▶ 9. My enthusiasm as a leader encourages others to be their best.

▶ 14. My enthusiasm as a leader creates an atmosphere of encouragement.

▶ 19. I do not whine or complain.

Think about a moment you felt incredibly enthusiastic: What generated that much enthusiasm, and how does that level of excitement compare to what you bring to your work or family every day? Coach had a passion and love for what he did, and he wanted his team to feel the same way. "Hard work without enthusiasm," Coach said, "leads to tedium. Enthusiasm without industriousness leads to unrealized potential. When combined, they cement a solid foundation."

_____

_____

_____

_____

THE FOUNDATION: SUPPORTING BLOCKS OF FRIENDSHIP, LOYALTY, AND COOPERATION

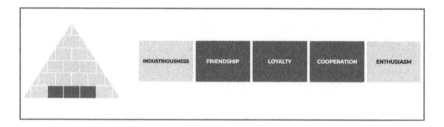

These three supporting, or "people" blocks, focus on others and reflect Coach's central belief that when we include others, we multiply our own strength and help us and them reach our full potential.

Friendship

Friendship comes from mutual esteem, respect, and devotion. Like marriage, it must not be taken for granted but requires a joint effort.

Friendship Assessment Statements:
- ▶ 1. I listen to the opinions of others before I offer my own opinion.
- ▶ 6. I have the respect of the people I work with.

- ► 11. I develop my professional relationships into genuine friendships.
- ► 16. I take the time to get to know others.

Coach maintained, "The time to make friends is before you need them." He knew his players would have differences and different opinions. The more they were brave enough to offer friendship first—to talk to each other, to do good things for another without expecting anything in return—those differences mattered less and less. Do you take the time to create quality relationships with your team? Are those relationships built on mutual esteem, respect, and devotion?

_____

_____

_____

_____

Loyalty

Have loyalty to yourself and to all those depending on you. Keep your self-respect.

Loyalty Assessment Statements:
- ► 2. Exercising proper judgment describes my approach to financial decisions.
- ► 7. I weather difficult times and grow stronger from them.
- ► 12. I would not intentionally betray another person.
- ► 17. You can tell from my life decisions that loyalty is one of my core values.

Is loyalty in the center of your strength as a coach and leader? How do you define it? For Coach, loyalty was made up of four virtues: devotion, commitment, duty, and faithfulness—to others (our business and people, family, job, teams, community, etc.) *and* yourself (your beliefs and values). You must have loyalty to yourself to have peace within. *Then* you must have loyalty to all those depending on you. Only then can you earn loyalty from others. As you grow in your devotion, commitment, duty, and faithfulness to each other, that loyalty enables you to get through difficult times.

_____

_____

_____

_____

Cooperation

Seek cooperation with all levels of the people you work with. Listen if you want to be heard. Be interested in finding the best way, not in having your own way.

Cooperation Assessment Statements:

> ▶ 3. I am more interested in finding the best way than having my own way.
> ▶ 8. I enjoy being involved in a healthy exchange of ideas about the most effective way to accomplish important tasks.
> ▶ 13. I move forward with a clear sense of direction.
> ▶ 18. I am cooperative when working with others.

Coach learned his first important lesson in cooperation by observing his father handling a team of horses trying to pull a heavy load out of a steep gravel pit: "Nothing is stronger than gentleness." Always strive to understand another's point of view and work together with others. As Coach said: "What is right is more important than who is right." That builds trust. Working *with* others always provides the opportunity to accomplish more than working alone. How do you look for cooperation from others or give your cooperation to others? Would others see your cooperation that way? What does it mean exactly to you when you say you trust your people? How do you set the example and teach that?

_____

_____

THE SECOND TIER: SELF-CONTROL, ALERTNESS, INITIATIVE, AND INTENTNESS

These blocks build on the strength and solidity of the foundation blocks.

Self-Control

Practice self-discipline and keep emotions under control. Good judgment and common sense are essential.

Self-Control Assessment Statements:
- ▶ 1. I maintain my composure during high-stress situations.
- ▶ 5. I maintain a positive attitude while serving others.
- ▶ 9. I accept personal accountability and monitor my behavior and performance.
- ▶ 13. At work and at home I follow the rules.

Think of a time at work or at home when you lost your self-control: What were the results? Likely not good. Any action or decision has a much greater chance to be workable and productive when done with self-control. Without self-discipline, you can't keep your emotions under control and maintain the delicate balance between mind and body.

Alertness

Be observing constantly. Stay open-minded. Be eager to learn and improve.

Alertness Assessment Statements:
- ► 4. I learn from my mistakes and strive to improve.
- ► 8. I am open-minded and adaptable, willing to take risks, fail, and grow.
- ► 12. I know of at least three ways I can improve.
- ► 16. I am aware of my strengths, and I am trying to improve my weaknesses.

Coach saw alertness as the key to anticipating the unexpected: seeing things before others see them and understanding what you're seeing, what it means, what actions must be taken or avoided, and what improvements can be made. He knew a coach needed the ability to see beyond what the team was doing on the court—what strategies were working, and what substitutions and adjustments had to be made. The same goes for coaching in the "game" of business and life: You need to focus simultaneously on what's in front of you and how it might affect what happens next. You can't have that alertness unless you are focused on others more than yourself. How in tune with others are you? What signals are you picking up from people in any situation that might help you orchestrate and better manage what is happening? Think about a time when you caught yourself saying "How did I miss that?" You have just given yourself a simple but effective alertness test. Now ask yourself, how could you have anticipated it or been aware enough to not miss it the next time?

_____

_____

_____

_____

Initiative

Cultivate the ability to make decisions and think alone. Do not be afraid of failure but learn from it.

Initiative Assessment Statements:
- ▶ 2. My vision and mission are clear.
- ▶ 6. I accept increasing amounts of responsibility.
- ▶ 10. I am confident in my decision-making ability.
- ▶ 14. I communicate with confidence and compassion.

As Coach said, "The man who is afraid to risk failure seldom has to face success. The only real failure is the failure to act when action is required." Preparation conquers fear, builds confidence, and fuels initiative, but even with all those things the road to success will be difficult. Don't let the difficulty deter the effort. You have probably said, "We learn from our mistakes, and we are always failing forward," but do you mean it? Do you put yourself in situations where failure is a real possibility? Or do you play it safe and opportunity is missed because initiative was stifled?

_____

_____

_____

_____

Intentness

Set a realistic goal. Concentrate on its achievement by resisting all temptations and being determined and persistent.

Intentness Assessment Statements:
- ▶ 3. I have a vision and goals for my life.
- ▶ 7. I am a patient person. I know good things take time.
- ▶ 11. I am not a quitter.

▶ 15. Helping others be successful provides purpose in my life and work.

Coach considered a realistic goal one that is not so idealistic that it becomes counterproductive when it isn't attained. He told himself and his players, "Do not permit what you cannot do to interfere with what you can do." Every goal must be difficult; things easily attained or achieved aren't meaningful or lasting. Intentness means having determination, persistence, and perseverance, extending everyone's capabilities to their limits to see how much they can truly accomplish together. As Bill Walton explained in *Wooden*, "[Coach] created an environment where you were expected to be your best and outscore the opponent, where capturing a championship and going undefeated was part of the normal course of events. Coach made the extraordinary seem normal. I can't describe how exciting it was to be a part of that—the joy he created in preparing us for competition."

THE HEART: CONDITION, SKILL, AND TEAM SPIRIT

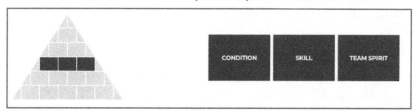

Coach called this the strongest tier of the Pyramid: Three blocks necessary to move near the peak—the key ingredients for success in sports and in life.

Condition

Mental, moral, and physical conditioning is necessary to be your best. Rest, exercise, and diet must be considered. Moderation must be practiced. Dissipation must be eliminated.

Condition Assessment Statements:

▶ 1. I take responsibility for developing the skills I need to perform my job to the best of my ability.

▶ 4. I balance the hours I spend at work and at home.

▶ 7. I possess a healthy moral, mental, and physical condition.

THE WISDOM OF WOODEN • THE WISDOM OF WOODEN • THE WISDOM OF WOODEN

THE IMPORTANCE OF CONDITION

The only psychological warfare John Wooden ever used on his opponents was the knowledge that his team was in better condition: "Never did I want to call the first time-out during a game. Never. It was almost a fetish with me because I stressed conditioning to such a degree. I wanted UCLA to come out and run our opponents so hard that they would be forced to call the first time-out just to catch their breath. I wanted them to have to stop the running before we did."

Coach's players accepted that responsibility—and the fact that even the best conditioned teams, like any team, can still fail. Even when Coach blamed himself for *not* calling a time-out. Years after he retired, he appeared on Charlie Rose with Bill Walton and said he was "haunted" by UCLA's double-overtime loss to North Carolina State in the 1974 NCAA Final Four. UCLA was ahead by seven with minutes to play and NC State came back, ending UCLA's streak of 38 consecutive NCAA tournament victories. Coach told Charlie Rose he "goofed" by not calling a time-out to rearrange his defense.

Walton quickly jumped to Coach's defense: "You weren't the reason we lost that game, Coach. We didn't need a time-out." Walton then explained to Rose that "a time-out was an admission of defeat and also that it gave the other team a chance to regroup."

▶ 10. I practice the fundamental aspects of my work to prepare for every challenge.

How do you think about the mental, moral, and physical condition of your team? Coach believed you could not attain peak physical condition unless it was preceded by mental *and* moral conditioning. Without proper conditioning in all areas, you will fall short of your potential.

_____

_____

_____

_____

Skill

A knowledge of and the ability to properly and quickly execute the fundamentals. Be prepared and cover every little detail.

Skill Assessment Statements:

▶ 3. I am a highly competent person.
▶ 6. I feel prepared to handle every little detail of my job.
▶ 9. I perform the tasks of my work quickly and properly.
▶ 12. My job performance has continued to improve.

Many large failures occur because of a lack of consistent execution of small fundamentals. Coach had gifted talent on his championship teams, but he knew even world-class skill improves gradually over time, which is why he required deliberate, hard practices that focused over and over on the fundamentals of the game. He covered every little detail so they could execute those fundamentals, properly and quickly, under increasingly challenging conditions. How clear are you on the most important fundamentals that drive the success of your life and business? Do you have a routine that enables you to continually improve those fundamentals?

_____

_____

_____

_____

Team Spirit

A genuine consideration for others. An eagerness to sacrifice personal interests of glory for the welfare of all.

Team Spirit Assessment Statements:

- ▶ 2. "Team player" is an appropriate description for me.
- ▶ 5. I sacrifice personal aspirations for the good of the team.
- ▶ 8. My attitude is positive.
- ▶ 11. I go out of my way to show appreciation for others.

Coach wanted people who were eager—not simply willing—to lose themselves in the group for the good of the group. Eagerness meant you *wanted* it. Sure, every player wanted to do well and receive praise, and Coach gave every one of them the love, consideration, dignity, and respect they deserved. He praised the assists, was quick to take blame, and gave credit where it was due. Then he demanded that they be eager to sacrifice their personal interests and desire for individual glory and put their skills to use for the good of the team. How do you and your team reflect this in your work and lives?

_____

_____

_____

_____

NEARING THE PEAK: POISE AND CONFIDENCE

Two blocks that are natural outcomes: You can't force them to happen; they happen naturally and habitually because of proper preparation and the experience gained from executing the blocks that support them.

Poise

Just being yourself. Being at ease in any situation. Never fighting yourself.

Poise Assessment Statements:
- ▶ 1. I learn from the leaders in my life and work.
- ▶ 3. I feel composed and ready for any situation that may occur at my job.
- ▶ 5. I handle crises calmly and without panic.
- ▶ 7. The only pressure I feel at work is the pressure I put on myself to do the best job I can.

Think about a situation where you may have tried to be someone you were not. How did it make you feel? Chances are, even if the results were good, you felt disconnected—uncomfortable in your own skin. Coach equated poise with the first of his father's Seven Point Creed: Be true to yourself. When you have poise, Coach said, "You're not acting. You're not pretending or trying to be something you're not. You are being who you are and are totally comfortable with that." If you have poise, you aren't overly concerned with what others think, your character is high, and outside forces won't change that or what you're trying to be, do, or become.

Confidence

Respect without fear. Confidence will come from being prepared and keeping all things in proper perspective.

Confidence Assessment Statements:
- ► 2. I am confident I could handle more responsibility.
- ► 4. I am proud of the work I produce.
- ► 6. I do my best work under high-pressure situations when the dead-line is drawing near.
- ► 8. I am confident but not arrogant.

Coach believed you earned the right to be proud and confident by working on all the behaviors and characteristics below it (and before it in the assessment). That confidence—in yourself and others—comes first and foremost from preparation and perspective. The tricky part is to maintain the fine line between confidence and overconfidence, avoiding self-centered, intimidating, or naive behavior.

THE PINNACLE: COMPETITIVE GREATNESS, FAITH, AND PATIENCE

Competitive Greatness provides the opportunity to demonstrate how all the qualities of the Pyramid's blocks come together. But Coach placed two blocks beside Competitive Greatness that he felt were essential for holding it up: Faith and Patience.

Competitive Greatness

Being at your best when your best is needed. Enjoyment of a difficult challenge.

Competitive Greatness Assessment Statements:

- ▶ 2. I enjoy tackling difficult issues at work because they challenge me to find creative solutions and perform at my highest levels of competency.
- ▶ 5. I have days that I would define as a "masterpiece."
- ▶ 8. I am a great competitor and enjoy a difficult challenge.
- ▶ 11. I am more focused on doing and becoming my best than I am on winning.

Coach and his teams found real joy and pleasure from being involved in something challenging. True competitors always do. They revel in it. There's little reward in doing the ordinary or something anyone can do. But the measure of true success is not the result on the scoreboard. The only measure is the answer to the question: Did I make the effort to do my best and maximize the potential of *everyone*? Look for opportunities to learn to rise to the occasion, improving ourselves and others as you do.

_____

_____

_____

_____

Faith

Faith (through prayer) is essential.

Faith Assessment Statements:
- ▶ 1. I believe things will work out for the best if I do the best I can.
- ▶ 4. I have faith that things will work out as they should, provided I do what I should.
- ▶ 7. I am confident that things will turn out as they should.
- ▶ 10. I make decisions that benefit others.

Coach memorized and often quoted what he felt was the most important lesson on faith in the Bible: "Faith is the substance of things hoped for, the evidence of things not seen" (Hebrews 11:1). Are you putting faith into just the things you can see? Or is your faith deeper and stronger than that? Faith to Coach meant having confidence in yourself *and* in something greater than yourself. He found his through prayer. Whatever you do, you must take responsibility for the development of your faith (no matter what that faith may be). To have faith, you must only believe things will turn out as they should, as long as you do what you should to help it become reality. It's a mature faith that comes from wisdom. That kind of faith takes time, which is why it stands next to Patience on the top of the Pyramid. So, why did Coach put Faith at the top of the Pyramid and not on the foundation? Because faith to him was about all the blocks below it: the effort you applied, the preparation you had done, the processes you created, and the experiences and failures you had and what you learned from them.

_____

_____

_____

_____

SOMETHING GREATER THAN YOURSELF

At the public launch of the first John R. Wooden Course in 2002, Lynn had planned on closing the program at the hotel ballroom with Swen Nater singing a version of "Wind Beneath My Wings," which he wrote especially for Coach. The packed room exploded in applause, just the way Lynn wanted the launch to end. Coach had another plan. The moment Swen finished, Coach said, "Tell Swen to sing another song." Lynn asked what song Coach wanted to hear, and he said, "His Eye Is on the Sparrow," a gospel hymn from 1905 and Coach's favorite. The song speaks to the idea that if a higher power is looking over the smallest of creatures, isn't it surely watching over us?

Swen was getting ready to leave the stage when Lynn told him, "Not so fast! Coach wants another song."

"What does Coach want to hear?" Swen asked, worried he wouldn't be able to play it. When he heard the selection was "His Eye Is on the Sparrow," he was delighted to be able to please Coach even more. He grinned, jumped up, and said, "I know that one!"

As Swen sang the first chorus, a small sparrow-like bird flew into the ballroom, took a lap around the room, then came to the front and hovered over Coach. All our eyes were on the sparrow as it lingered until Swen finished and then, as if on cue, flew out of the room. Lynn knows that sounds impossible or at least scripted for a hotel event so close to Hollywood. But Lynn had nothing to do with it. It happened, and faith that there is something greater than yourself was in that moment. You don't need to worship in any particular way to recognize what Coach knew and experienced: When it comes to faith, there are higher powers at work in your life, which will give you, like it gave Lynn with the Wooden Course and Coach's legacy, the encouragement and guidance that you need just when you need it to believe in and stay with what you are being called to do. And that calling is bigger than you are.

Patience

Good things take time—and they should!

Patience Assessment Statements:

- ▶ 3. I realize that not all things are under my control, so my circumstances do not define my attitude.
- ▶ 6. I take the time to make the best decisions.
- ▶ 9. I am calm and patient when projects, tasks, or events take longer than I expect.
- ▶ 12. I realize it takes a long time to create excellence.

Coach would never mistake activity for achievement. He believed becoming your best is a process of ups and downs, challenging setbacks, and exhilarating accomplishments. That was true about all his success. It took Coach two years to write his definition of success, 14 years to complete his Pyramid of Success, and almost 20 years coaching to win his first championship. He knew if he was going to appreciate what he had accomplished, those things should have taken time. Patience is also a by-product of solitude, silence, and stillness. Not all change is progress, but there is no progress without change. How do you set the example of this for your team?

_____

_____

MORTAR: THE STRENGTH OF HUMAN CHARACTER (SINCERITY, HONESTY, RELIABILITY, INTEGRITY)

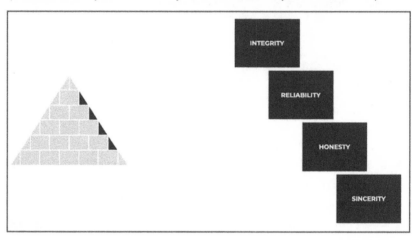

The four mortar blocks on the right form "The Strength of Human Character": Four ideals that encompass the authenticity, power, and influence of human character.

Sincerity

Makes and keeps friends.

Sincerity Assessment Statements:
- ▶ 2. My communication style is direct and positive.
- ▶ 6. I am an authentic person.
- ▶ 10. I am a sincere person.
- ▶ 14. I act in a thoughtful and selfless way toward others.

Sincerity is the glue of Friendship, Loyalty, Cooperation, and Team Spirit. Sincerity in you is a catalyst for helping others bring out their best. Would your team call you sincere? Would they remember an occasion in which you acted in a thoughtful and selfless way toward them?

_____

_____

_____

_____

Honesty

In thoughts and actions must occur at all times and in all ways.

Honesty Assessment Statements:
- ▶ 1. I do not intentionally mislead others.
- ▶ 5. I say what I mean and mean what I say.
- ▶ 9. I am trustworthy.
- ▶ 13. I take responsibility for my mistakes and make the best effort to improve my performance.

You feel good about when you are honest, even when the truth hurts. By being dishonest, you destroy your credibility and reputation and lose your self-respect, not to mention the respect of others. Tell the truth! As Coach said, "That way you don't have to remember a story."

_____

_____

_____

_____

Reliability

Others depend on us to give our best effort.

Reliability Assessment Statements:
- ▶ 4. I am reliable.

▶ 8. I ask for help when I am having difficulty completing a task.

▶ 12. I can depend on others to help me in difficult situations.

▶ 16. I trust other people who can impact my success.

When coupled with capability, reliability is a powerful force in all your relationships. That reliability comes from showing up in those relationships—consistently! You create and earn respect through that consistency. That's the only way for others to understand your expectations for their reliability and how you depend on them. Your own self-discipline and enthusiasm to do the things you're responsible for when you say you will set the example of the reliability you expect from the people you are leading and coaching. How are you doing this? Who taught you the importance of reliability, and how did they do it? Was there a time when your reliability was less than it should have been, and you let somebody down who you cared about?

Integrity

Holds up Competitive Greatness with purity of intention.

Integrity Assessment Statements:

▶ 3. I live my life in an ethical manner.

▶ 7. I never take credit for work I didn't perform.

▶ 11. My behavior reflects the highest levels of integrity.

▶ 15. I admire the people I work with for the conviction of their beliefs.

Coach's quest for the peace of mind essential to his definition of success came one day at a time, one night at a time. Day to day, he lived his life mindful of the quality of his conscience and his character. He used to say, "There's no pillow softer than a clear conscience." You must never sacrifice your morals or values whatever they are. You must strive to act with goodness, character, dignity, and genuine concern about the betterment of others. Anyone who does this possesses a clear conscience. How soft is your pillow?

_____

_____

_____

_____

MORTAR: THE FORCE OF THE HUMAN SPIRIT (AMBITION, ADAPTABILITY, RESOURCEFULNESS, FIGHT)

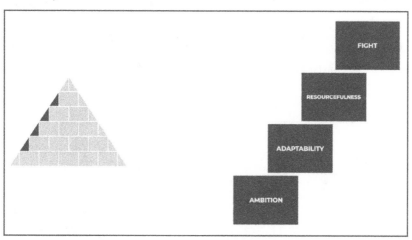

The triangular blocks along the sides of the Pyramid are the mortar that connect and hold things in place. They reflect how you keep things glued together, because without mortar, the whole structure would crumble. The four mortar blocks on the left form "The Force of the Human Spirit": Four ideals that build from the foundation up and encompass the strength, tenacity, and stamina of the human spirit.

_____

_____

_____

_____

Ambition

Must be properly focused on noble and worthy purposes.

Ambition Assessment Statements:
- ▶ 4. I am motivated to accomplish my work and goals.
- ▶ 8. I discern between urgent and important matters because my priorities are clear.
- ▶ 12. I refuse to compromise my ethical standards in my pursuit of success.
- ▶ 16. I am driven to achieve my goals.

The most noble and worthy purposes are focused on bringing others along on the journey of success. You must never, however, let ambition cause you to sacrifice your integrity or diminish your efforts on any aspect of the Pyramid.

_____

_____

_____

_____

Adaptability

Sees change as constant and inevitable in any and every situation.

Adaptability Assessment Statements:
- ▶ 2. When I make mistakes, I recognize the error and work quickly to invent a solution to the problem at hand.
- ▶ 6. I am flexible enough to meet the challenges created by changes in my life and work.

> ► 10. I have a healthy and proper respect for authority.
> ► 14. I look for better ways to do things.

Failing to adapt is failing to move forward. Grow with it. Learn from it and by it. But heed what Coach said, "Although there is no progress without change, not all change is progress."

_____

_____

_____

_____

Resourcefulness

Shows proper judgment and provides capital for an entrepreneurial spirit that can be invested for greater gains.

Resourcefulness Assessment Statements:

> ► 3. No matter the situation, I find a way to do my best.
> ► 7. I am a creative problem-solver.
> ► 11. I use the resources that I have been given.
> ► 15. I see challenging circumstances not as problems but as opportunities to test my abilities, learn, and grow.

The human mind is the most wonderful weapon for overcoming adversity. Use it to apply common sense *and* invent solutions to whatever problems you must overcome and whatever goals you seek to achieve. Think how those greater gains could benefit others.

_____

_____

_____

_____

Fight

Holds up Competitive Greatness with determined effort to do the best we can do.

Fight Assessment Statements:
- ▶ 1. I am ready to move when the opportunity arises.
- ▶ 5. I do things quickly, but I don't hurry.
- ▶ 9. I stand my ground and remain true to what I believe is right.
- ▶ 13. I disagree without being disagreeable.

As Coach said, "Goals achieved with little effort are seldom worthwhile or lasting." Stand your ground, grit your teeth, and dig in. Hustle! Be ready to move when opportunity arises. Be quick but don't hurry. Know how and when to play hurt, and when not to play injured. Not just getting up for the "big game" but getting up for every game—and for others. And remember: The fight must be within, never with another.

_____

_____

_____

_____

THE WOODEN WAY WORKsheet

Reflect on Your Assessment

Note: The online assessment gives you access to a 30-day action plan for improving yourself based on each block of the Pyramid. You can replicate the online plan by answering the questions below and in the following chapter, as well as returning to each block of the Pyramid and reflecting on how you will improve, maintain, and sustain your work on it.

THE WOODEN WAY WORKsheet

How accurately do you feel the assessment reflected how you see your day-to-day behavior at work and in your life?

_____

_____

_____

Looking back, were there any major surprises or "aha" moments?

_____

_____

_____

What was the most important thing you learned about yourself by taking the assessment?

_____

_____

_____

What steps would you like to take next in your personal development journey?

_____

_____

_____

Coach said, "If we magnified blessings as much as we magnify disappointments, we would all be much happier." Keeping that in

THE WOODEN WAY WORKsheet

mind, look at the top scores in your assessment. Where do they cluster? How do you understand the implications of those areas in your life and others' lives, and the opportunity they give you to make an impact? What can you do more to put these things to work?

_____

_____

_____

Now go to the bottom: What can you do to think through those lower scores a little more? Where do they cluster? How does that make you feel? Do a little journaling in those areas as you ask yourself the question: Why did I score myself the way I did in those blocks and tiers, and where are my opportunities to improve in them?

_____

_____

_____

Finally, go back to Chapters 3 and 4 and consider what you wrote:

- ▶ as your three legacy words,
- ▶ as your fundamentals and foundations, and
- ▶ as your definition of success.

THE WOODEN WAY WORKsheet

How are those answers reflected in the Pyramid and your assessment? Do you feel differently about them now? Why or why not?

_____

_____

_____

FIND YOUR COACH!

"I'd need many more fingers and toes to count the number of times I have
not been home on time. I could probably count on just my fingers the
number of times I've ever been late to work. It's way out of balance."

This was Jason's "aha moment" when reviewing his individual
assessment with Lynn. Much of their conversation had been engaging
and insightful—a reflection of who Jason was now and how he thought
about things. Lynn had reviewed how strong Jason was on the mortar of
the Pyramid, especially the character blocks and competitive greatness,
yet he found himself lacking when it came to poise and just being himself.
But the real focus was on why and how Jason scored himself lower on
the foundation of the Pyramid. In fact, his lowest scores on the entire
assessment were industriousness and friendship.

"Why did you score yourself like that?" Lynn asked, pointing out
Jason's struggles with planning out his day. That was when Jason had
his moment. "A real zinger," he said. It resonated with him deeply. He
remembered that he had recently rewatched Coach's TED Talk (Coach
was 91 at the time). In that talk, Coach spoke about the importance of
planning, of never going over in his schedule and always being home on
time. But Jason only connected those dots with Lynn when reviewing the
assessment.

"Coach always spoke about his disciplined approach to the management
of all his time and every task. It could be his meeting with his coaches,

practice, five-mile lunchtime walk around the UCLA track, or family dinner," Lynn said. "Every day was well organized. He had that rigor and self-discipline at work and at home. Seems like you could use some of that."

"I have not gotten home on time," Jason repeated. "You're right, that's a reflection of poor planning and prioritization. Industriousness is about careful planning and hard work, and I work hard. But my score is skewed by the low score I gave myself on planning. I'm capable of keeping a schedule and following a plan. I perform poorly at that in comparison to what I do well. What would add to my productivity and improve other things would be the ability to organize and plan my day and stick with my plan. And then get home to my family on time too."

"So, what are your next steps?" Lynn asked.

"Spend time thinking about the things that would produce the results and changes I need to make. There's lots of grace at home for being late. There is not a lot of grace for missing a deadline at work. But why always dip into that savings account of grace?" Jason replied.

"What you've realized is the Pyramid sets a very high standard, and your gut and your scores tell you that you are falling short in areas that are really important to you and to your family," Lynn added. "That lack of planning affected your friendship score too. Friendship is right next to industriousness on the Pyramid. That means you have to work at friendship to make friendship flourish. You need a plan to invest your time there also—and you need to stick to that plan. It has to be intentional."

Jason's talk with Lynn reinforced what he had learned since his first conversation with Lynn about working with GoldenComm: The Wooden Way is a team sport, and every team needs a coach. You can't get there on your own, especially if your ultimate goal is to bring others along on that journey to becoming your best. The discussions you need to have now and moving forward with the Wooden Coaching Model and the five lessons that follow in the Wooden Way are not going to happen by reading or watching anything or conversations with yourself. They work best when shared with someone who serves as a coach for you.

Note we said "coach" not "Coach," as in John Wooden. Jason's aha moment came when talking with Lynn about the assessment, not listening to Coach's TED Talk on the same subject or reading the descriptions of the Pyramid's blocks. Lynn's aha moments of success came from working with Coach as his coach. Thanks to that relationship, Coach's wisdom is the beacon of this book. But Coach is not here for us now physically, just as we cannot be there for every reader of this book. We can share our stories and Coach's, along with his timeless wisdom, life lessons, and legacy. We cannot be there to coach you as you use the assessment and all we have covered. *You* must recognize the need for change, be motivated to change, develop the ability to change, and be prompted to make the changes that lead not just to improvement but the opportunity to realize your greatest potential. A good coach can move you along in all those areas. A great coach can make all the difference in helping you complete your journey to both greatness and goodness.

Simply put, it's dialogue between humans that creates transformation. So, before proceeding to Part II, invite at least one other person on your journey. Find a great coach who can not only coach you but help model how you coach others.

THE WOODEN WAY WORKsheet

Find Your Coach

No, seriously: Share! The opportunity to share your assessment and talk to others and build a coaching community around the Pyramid—for self-coaching and coaching yourself way up—cannot be understated. Write down at least one person who you will share the assessment with and one person you want to take the assessment. Discuss it with each other honestly and openly. Schedule it. Plan for it. Give it the time it deserves and keep at it. Build a group with people who offer different experiences and know you from different parts of your life or keep it one-on-one but build your community by finding at least one coach to coach you way up!

THE WOODEN WAY WORKsheet

When you're ready, consider building something bigger and forming a "Pyramid Partner Group"—a mastermind-like group in which everyone works together to coach each other way up on each block of The Pyramid of Success. Here is our five-point checklist for considering and applying each block as you have those coaching conversations:

1. Make It Personal: Change and improve *you* first.

2. Make It Practical: Start small and move to bigger things only after you are successful with smaller things. (Like the Japanese concept of *kaizen*: Small steps can add up to big improvements.)

3. Make It Possible: Don't just *feel* you can do this—you need to *know* you can do this. See the beginning, the progression, and the completion.

4. Make It Provable: Lay out what and when you will accomplish what you set out to do.

5. Make It Powerful: Know what you're doing will make a difference.

Remember: Success as you define it is what you are working toward for yourself and your business now. The lessons ahead in the Wooden Way on thinking, setting the example, teaching, leading, and mentoring are how you build on your definition of success and learn to be the coach and person you want and need to be.

PART II

Five Lessons
for Leading

How do I execute better as a coach and a leader?

Understanding the results of your assessment using The Pyramid of Success helped you take the important first step for self-evaluation (recognizing the need for change) and provided a starting point for you to examine your values and behavior. However, like the Great Pyramid of Giza that was Coach Wooden's inspiration, The Pyramid of Success has a flaw: It's static. It contains a definition of what Coach meant by the term "success," and answers the question "What behaviors are needed to achieve success?" But without any direction as to what to do first, next, or at all when it comes to bringing each block to life, to get better and be your best, it has left people like Jason and his team asking "Now what?"

People connect magnificently with the ideals of the Pyramid because it is so fundamentally sound, logical, and full of simple truths. Moreover, its definitions are clear, and the relationships between each block are enlightening. That's why Jason and his team hung pictures of each block of the Pyramid around the office at GoldenComm to remind them to keep thinking about them and what they meant.

But after taking their assessments and understanding the results, Coach's story, and the Pyramid bottom to top, Jason and his team had a question: *Are we going to just keep talking about the Pyramid or do something about it? How do we put it into action and get better?* Which was their way of saying "Now what?"

The five lessons of the Wooden Way answer that question. Part I used the Wooden Coaching Model to find and test the coach in you. Part II puts you on the path of becoming the leader you need to be to coach yourself and your team way up.

These lessons are based on the philosophy Coach articulated in the first—and only—book he wrote on his own: *Practical Modern Basketball* (1966). The book remains a master course on all aspects of the game of basketball and powerful lessons for coaching life. It captures the disciplined way Coach thought about the processes and systems he believed in and employed but, true to his beliefs, focuses his strategies and tactics as much on the development of the person as the player—starting with himself.

Coach knew being successful at one point in your life was no guarantee of success at a later point. You don't stop when you get close or achieve your goal; that's limiting. His goal was perfection, but it was an ongoing process—even when his teams reached it (four times) on the court. He knew he must stay on the Pyramid to finish strong and continue to grow.

That's why, until the day he died, Coach always worked on the quality of his *thinking* and to *set the example, teach, lead,* and *mentor* others. Those *words* make up the five lessons of the Wooden Way.

Five Lessons for Leading the Wooden Way

 ### How You Think

Seek wisdom—understand how the quality of your thinking determines the quality of your philosophy about the fundamentals that guide your work and life.

 ### How You Set the Example

Demonstrate clarity and consistency in the attitude, actions, and behavior you model and expect your team to follow.

 ### How You Teach

Teach by setting the example and using preparation, effort, methodology, and commitment to create healthy habits that instinctively produce excellence under ever increasing pressure.

 ### How You Lead

Encouraging individuals to work together for the common good and the best possible results, while at the same time letting them know they did it themselves.

 ## How You Mentor

Harness the power in mentoring to improve yourself and to serve those you have the privilege to help develop.

Coach never stopped building the greatness and goodness within himself and those he had the privilege to help develop. He never stopped trying to improve his ability to do the things that set him apart. The more you understand what that means to you as you coach and master the principles within these five lessons, the more you can affect real change, be a difference maker, and the best coach and leader you can be for your family and your business.

"You must be
interested in finding
the best way, not in having
your own way."

CHAPTER 7

Lesson One: How You Think

"Don't let the GPS take you into the Pacific Ocean." That's Jason's line about thinking or, rather, the lack thereof. A GPS is a useful tool for navigation, but you can't let it think for you. A GPS also doesn't know who you are, and it can't teach you how to drive, see the other people in your car and those driving around you, or know why you are going where you're going.

Neither can The Pyramid of Success. It's a powerful tool for thinking about your behavior and maintaining that behavior as you navigate the road ahead. But it can't think for you. Coach spent 14 years thinking about the Pyramid before settling on its final form. But it was still only a GPS for him and the quality of his thinking, just as it was for Jason after working with Lynn. That "now what?" question Jason and his team asked? That's where Coach's Pyramid and wisdom needed to become their guide—tools for assessing and navigating their thinking and actions for moving forward.

That's also where Lesson One: How You Think comes into play: *Seek wisdom—understand how the quality of your thinking determines the quality of your philosophy about the fundamentals that guide your work and life.* In this chapter, you will complete the lesson by assessing the quality of your thinking, articulating your leadership philosophy, and developing a "to-think list."

ASSESS THE QUALITY OF YOUR THINKING

Lynn and Coach often talked about that time in his coaching development when Lynn's hometown hero was winning a championship at Ohio State and Coach hadn't yet gotten the talent to really compete at the national level. He told Lynn he would have loved to coach players like Lucas, Havlicek, and Siegfried at Ohio State. But he knew, even when he got players of that caliber, talent alone was not enough to compete—not without maximum effort, careful planning, rigorous attention to detail, precise execution of the most essential fundamentals, and total commitment to the team concept. And Coach knew his team's performance and productivity started with the quality of his thinking. He had to focus his mind, organize and plan his daily activities, and follow through on doing them. Everything in Coach's day-to-day improvement process started with the quality of thinking (both his own and his coaches and players) and how today and the next days could be improved using his Pyramid of Success.

How do you think about making changes in your life and business? Look at Figure 7–1 on page 113 to see how Coach spoke and thought about the process of change and his need to constantly assess and work on the quality of his thinking lest he get stuck in the status quo. Think about this in terms of how you think about change.

- ▶ *Status Quo.* "Not all change is progress, but there is no progress without change." Coach recognized his life was always about change, but change did not mean breaking free from the status quo. He was always mindful of the changes he needed to make in his program, his people, and his life to move forward, starting with how he was thinking.

- ▶ *Right Thinking.* "People are usually as happy as they make up their minds to be." Coach learned from his parents, who raised their children through difficult circumstances, that being optimistic and

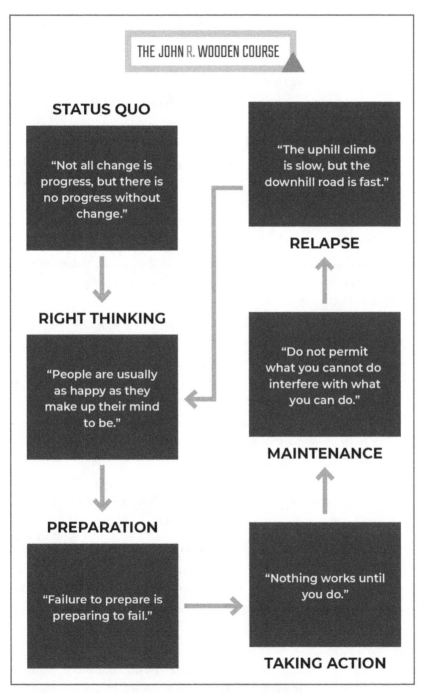

FIGURE 7–1 *How John Wooden Thought About Change*

happy and having a positive attitude was a choice. Coach made the same choice about his thinking, especially when it came to change. If he wasn't positive, optimistic, and happy about the change, he wasn't thinking right.

▶ *Preparation.* "Failure to prepare is preparing to fail." Once Coach felt he was thinking right, he prepared for how and when the changes should be made. He considered the solutions he was working toward. What might the obstacles be? What would he and the team have to give up to pursue the change? Who he would need to help him execute the change?

▶ *Taking Action.* "Nothing works until you do." Coach tested and tried things, but ultimately he thought about the actions he was determined to take to make the change possible and successful. Then, he took those actions *and* took responsibility for teaching and leading the team through them.

▶ *Maintenance.* "Do not permit what you cannot, do interfere with what you can." Coach knew that staying on course after making a change required as much work as making the change in the first place. He kept working on the course of action knowing he was going to fall back or even fail.

▶ *Relapse.* "The uphill climb is slow, but the downhill road is fast." Coach never questioned his thinking too soon. He refused to make small setbacks bigger than they had any right to be. But when the change had run its course (or failure was apparent) and his thinking needed to evolve or be replaced, he worked on his "right thinking" and started over to avoid getting stuck in the status quo.

The quality of Coach's thinking set the tone for his feelings, determined the correctness of his behavior, and defined the course of his actions—for himself and as the leader of his team. His mind was not cluttered by spending time thinking about himself, worrying what others thought about him, or comparing himself with others (let alone trying to be better than them). He knew if he was not thinking correctly, not much good would follow. Instead, his thinking was driven by an insatiable appetite to learn and improve his abilities to teach and make a difference in the lives of others. The challenge for you as a coach is to do the same.

So, what does that mean? In the first chapter of *Practical Modern Basketball*, Coach defined a high-quality thinker as someone who puts in the effort to:

- meet all events whether favorable or unfavorable with calmness and composure.
- have a love of wisdom and knowledge.
- study the processes governing thought and conduct.
- know the general principles or laws of a field of knowledge or activity.
- study human morals, character, and behavior.

That said, Coach was constantly testing his capability too. He believed there were no real secrets to the "game," at least not for long. He knew if he got stuck in one way (his way) or the past, he couldn't evolve his thinking and find the best way. There are *always* good ways and better ways to do things. There are always others who can do things better or see different opportunities than you in the game and in life. What are they thinking

THE WISDOM OF WOODEN • THE WISDOM OF WOODEN • THE WISDOM OF WOODEN

EVOLVE YOUR THINKING

Basketball was a control sport when Coach took his first job at Indiana State in 1946. In *Practical Modern Basketball*, he recalled how he eventually chose to adapt to the fast-paced style of the other teams, because the fans liked it and it was fun to watch. An entertaining bad team might also buy him another year on the job where a boring bad team might not.

But while he never had a losing record as a college basketball coach and even made the NCAA tournament a few times, Coach never came close to winning a championship until his 16th season, when his Walt Hazzard–led team made the 1962 NCAA Final Four. After getting so close for the first time, Coach didn't think, "I've got this figured out. Wait 'til next year!" He knew success the following year was no guarantee—even with great play-ers—without a culture and system to match. He had the culture. He needed a better system. So, Coach got back on his Pyramid of Success and re-evaluated *everything*. He rebuilt the offense. Developed new plays. Added a press. Shortened practice. The result? After posting a better regular season record than the previous year, UCLA lost to Arizona State in the second round of the 1963 tournament by 14 points. This time, however, Coach liked what he saw, and he went to work refining and improving it for 1964—the first of his ten championships in 12 years.

about? What do they know that you don't? How can you learn from them to improve your thinking? Every year Coach took on a summer project to improve his thinking and what he did in a certain part of the game, or in a certain part of his life. The "trick" is to find the best way with the goal of perfection always in mind. Being satisfied (i.e., complacency) is always your enemy. You must firmly believe in what you are doing and that it is not what you do as much as how well you do it based on sound thinking.

Coach's father shared a short poem when Coach was young about the importance of clear thinking. That poem by the Reverend Henry Van Dyke had a lifelong influence, particularly the opening line: "Four things a man must learn to do if he would make his life more true: To think without confusion clearly."

Your first exercise in this lesson is to consider whether you are thinking "without confusion clearly" and if you need to make a shift in your thinking— first by assessing the quality of the input you are working with, then by considering the priorities for your thinking. The frequency, speed, and sheer quantity of information available to us today is mind-boggling compared to when Coach led, which makes his lessons on the importance of the quality, consistency, clarity, and soundness of your thinking even more applicable. What are the most important things on your mind? How are you thinking about yourself and others? It takes discipline and constant practice to separate the noise from the information, data/facts, knowledge, and especially wisdom.

THE WOODEN WAY WORKsheet

Assess Your Thinking

How is your thinking being most influenced today? By what and whom?

_____

_____

_____

How do you feel about those sources? Are they preparing you to handle your most important challenges and opportunities in work and in life? If they are, in what ways? Be specific. If not, how can you shift your thinking?

_____

_____

_____

Once you have shifted your thinking about the quality of your input, think about your life professionally *and* personally—the people you lead and the relationships you have. Is your thinking driving your day-to-day actions in a way that is best serving those who are depending on you? Is it improving the quality of those relationships and the things you can accomplish together?

_____

_____

_____

ARTICULATE YOUR LEADERSHIP PHILOSOPHY

The first chapter of *Practical Modern Basketball* is called "My Coaching Philosophy." But Coach did not want coaches and leaders to use that chapter to think like him. He wanted to demonstrate how his philosophy informed all he did so others could use it as a guide for developing their own. To him, great coaches were *unique* thinkers capable of strategizing effective solutions to difficult challenges over and over.

Coach believed it was a necessity for any coach to have a philosophy of their own if only to react in a philosophical way to all the unpredictable reactions of people who believe they have some stake in the outcome of a contest or situation. As a coach, you must recognize that you will be placed in a position of public view (with your people, vendors, and clients) and may even at times receive unjustifiable criticism and undeserved praise. You must not be unduly affected by either. Instead you need to think about the right things, the right ways, at the right times, for the right reasons, and have a clear, compelling vision of the results that could be shared and taught. But you need your own coaching philosophy to guide that vision.

The importance Coach placed on having a philosophy continues to impact coaches today—even successful ones. For example, at the 2017 Postback marketing and tech conference, Pete Carroll, the Super Bowl-winning coach of the Seattle Seahawks, asked the audience how many of them could recite their personal leadership philosophy. Carroll then told the crowd he had learned the importance of having a philosophy from John Wooden. It was Coach who told Carroll, long before Carroll's team won the Super Bowl, that he was good at coaching, but if he wanted to be a great coach, he needed to have a philosophy and make it clear to everyone he led: "[W]hat hit me is that he had this philosophy," Carroll said. "He knew what he thought, and it wasn't like anybody else. . . . If you want to be great, if you want to do something really at the top of your game, you got to figure out who you are, what you stand for, what's important. And not even that, so you can convey it to the people around you, so they know about it."

Carroll got Coach perfectly right, but one wonders how many people in the audience would still have their hands up if he had asked if they had that philosophy written down for everyone to see. Coach always said if your philosophy is not written down, you can't consistently, clearly, and correctly articulate what it is. If your people can't see it, how can you expect them to follow it?

You're the "head coach" of the people you serve and are responsible for. Without articulating your leadership philosophy—starting with your core values—you and they have no compass for making the tough decisions and leading through the most uncertain and challenging of circumstances.

Your leadership philosophy is your best thinking, your lighthouse through everything business and life throws at you. It will and should be tested and can evolve. But if it's unstated, unclear, or constantly changing with every impulse, exception, fad, or the hot leadership "flavor of the month," you will fast find yourself with a team of individuals, rather than individuals working together as a team. It must be one team, one philosophy, one core set of values, and one destination. For Coach Wooden, that destination was always "to be the best we can be." Without that, you can still be successful like Pete Carroll was before he met Coach, but your "team" will be more about individual talent than commitment, cooperation, consistency, and excellence. You may have a winning year or two, but you'll never be able to get on the track to sustained excellence.

When your philosophy is clear, your people have boundaries but can still have their own identities as they do their jobs, always adding value and solving for what you need them to do. There doesn't need to be one way to do things for everyone. You just need strength in the Pyramid's Foundation (industriousness, friendship, loyalty, cooperation, and enthusiasm)—especially cooperation where the leader must set the bar high when it comes to "being more interested in finding the best way than in having your own way." The "my way or the highway" leader will not likely get the cooperation needed or the results desired to take their team to extraordinary levels of sustained performance. Every player and every position matter. For example, Jason has a "Swen Nater" position at GoldenComm—the role-playing backup that pushes his all-stars. He has people who would rather work 40 hours a week around coaching youth sports, spending time with their kids, surfing, or going to Bible study. He also has people want to work 80 hours a week and surpass all the

THE WOODEN WAY WORKsheet

Your Philosophy

When coaches came to Coach and asked what they needed to do to turn their careers around or reach the next level, he always started by having them think about the quality of their thinking: What do you want to do as a coach? What do you stand for? What do you want to ultimately accomplish in the game—for the team, the organization, and especially in the lives of your team members? How are your players getting along? What are you trying to establish in the locker room? How are you thinking about the values that surround and influence the team? Who are the players that best embody your philosophy? Who are the players that behave inconsistently based on your philosophy?

Thus, your second exercise in this lesson is to articulate your coaching and leadership philosophy.

What is your philosophy as a coach and leader? What do you stand for? (If you need help, turn to the words on The Pyramid of Success as your guide.)

_____

_____

_____

_____

_____

_____

_____

THE WOODEN WAY WORKsheet

Identify the three most important things you want your team thinking about every day.

1. _____

2. _____

3. _____

Now, ask yourself: Does your team know everything you just wrote? If you called any of your team members right now and asked them what your philosophy is and to connect it to the core values of your company, could they answer?

---

company's productivity goals and earn more. And that's OK, as long as they are following the Pyramid *and* the philosophy of GoldenComm. For the latter, they look to Jason.

DEVELOP A "TO-THINK" LIST

Individuals look to you for leadership, guidance, and boundaries. You can't make up those boundaries as you go, but you must be willing to constantly assess them. That's where Jason was at the end of his story that opened this book.

Before he met Lynn, Jason had already had several leaders in his life challenge him on his thinking: Diane (who compelled him to change the quality of his input when he was just reading the baseball box scores each morning) and Ankur (who challenged him to give up the proprietary GC Lead Machine that didn't work for his team and cost him employees).

Following Ankur's inspiration, Jason challenged his leadership philosophy, specifically GoldenComm's core values, which he called

"Jason's Way": learn, change, grow, do, and serve. If he owed it to his people to mainstream the proprietary part of the company's products, then he felt he owed them a voice in thinking about and then owning the values they all would work and live by. Jason didn't want his way; he wanted the *best way.*

To start the process, Jason needed only to follow the advice he gives his clients: "We create 'websites that work harder' to provide some form of return for our clients: save them time, bring them leads, make them money, better service their clients. . . . If they are a new company, I will tell my clients to lead with their products and services.

"If they are an established company, I will tell them to lead with their principles and values. We are an established company. So, we had to lead with our principles and values. Any teenager can build a website. What is the value that we offer? We are purpose, principle, and value driven. That's how we think. Our systems and process support how we get there. What are the core values that support that? I wanted to get our leadership team to own that philosophy with me, so it wasn't just about me."

With Lynn as his coach and The Pyramid of Success as his GPS, Jason asked himself the hard questions, then put them to his team:

- ▶ How am I thinking about the business every day?
- ▶ What are the things I would want my people to be thinking about every day?
- ▶ How do all of us think about the work we are doing, the clients we are serving, and how we cooperate and work together as a team?

Lynn then led Jason and his group through the John R. Wooden Course and the blocks of the Pyramid as they thought about those questions and what else constitutes quality thinking at GoldenComm.

"We talked about business acumen," Jason recalls. "We had been building websites since 1996 at GoldenComm; we understand how businesses make money on the web and how to put our knowledge in the service of their clients' businesses. We talked about service in terms of responsiveness and how clients feel when they work with us: Do they feel like they're being 'handled' or served as people by us with empathy for what they need?

"We talked about grit but not just as it applies to intentness and goals. There's a lot of important things you must do at GoldenComm that the clients can't understand and never see. It's hard to do things that are 'invisible' to anyone but us. It's hard when you never get a 'Wow!' from a client. That takes grit because you have to do all these things and never get acknowledged. We talked about transparency; how we tell people everything that they want to know about what we do and how it isn't magic. We talked about the technical ability or skill behind the business acumen. We talked about how we all worked hard to contribute to the whole no matter our experience or time served."

In the end, those things the GoldenComm team discussed became the six core values for the company to align around top to bottom: *service, business acumen, grit, technical ability, transparency, and hard work.* But just like the Pyramid blocks that hang around GoldenComm with those core values, that writing on the wall and all the thinking behind them would not add up to much if Jason failed to set the example and live by those blocks and values.

Which brings us to the second lesson in this part of the Wooden Way for coaching yourself and your team way up: Most people have a "to-do" list, but do you have a "to-think" list? The hard work and careful planning at the core of the industriousness cornerstone of The Pyramid of Success is about thinking as much as action. Tap into the power of your brain and the "resourcefulness" block to think and not just act with common sense and proper judgment. Your brain is the most powerful tool in your arsenal for responding to opportunities with solutions and solving the problems that can keep you from being your best. We do so many things on our "to-do" lists just by inertia like we are brushing our teeth—we get so ingrained in them, we don't even think about what they are doing. All behavior change/improvement starts with the thinking needed to clarify the aspiration to improve. Better thinking will result in you considering better behavior options.

THE WOODEN WAY WORKsheet

Create Your "To-Think" List

Your final exercise in this lesson is to start a daily habit by creating your "to-think" list: a challenge to begin every day *thinking about your thinking*. Where do you think better thinking in your work and in your life could have a positive impact? Pick one area that if improved could have immediate impact. Consider your attitude. How could your attitude be improved? Start small: Identify one situation where a better attitude would have created a better situation and or a better outcome. It all starts with your thinking.

_____

_____

_____

_____

Once you have done this for yourself, start working with and challenging your coaches (i.e., leadership team) and "players" to complete the same process. You want them to think about the quality of their thinking when it comes to attitude and action. Can you picture your team starting every day focused on thinking about the things that should be on their minds and guiding their actions and performance? Bring them together like Jason did, and use the Pyramid to think hard about your core values and how they connect to your attitude, actions, and behaviors.

"No written word nor spoken plea can teach our youth what they should be. Nor all the books on all the shelves. It's what the teachers are themselves."

CHAPTER 8

Lesson Two:
How You Set the Example

Imagine John Wooden arriving at UCLA in 1948. After compiling a two-year record of 44–15 at Indiana State, he had been widely recruited from the Midwest hotbed of college basketball. He chose UCLA and became only the fourth coach in the school's history. And with that he walks into his new home . . . a crappy men's gym known across campus as the "B.O. Barn." White dust covered the floor—chalk residue from the women's gymnastics team practice on the other side of the curtain that ran down the middle of the floor. Coach had been promised a new field house in a few years to match the quality of the players he planned to recruit, but the ones he had inherited were in as poor condition as the gym. Anyone might have asked "What have I gotten myself into?" But Coach simply got started. He picked up a mop and bucket and started cleaning the dust off the floor.

Preparation, planning, time put in, and a level of intensity in everything Coach did represented one side of his industriousness (a cornerstone of the Pyramid). The other side, of equal importance especially when setting the example for his team, was his MBA: Mop and Bucket Attitude. To Coach, no job was too small, unimportant, or menial—*every* detail mattered—when it came to making the environment a better place for his players to play and demonstrating the character he demanded of them. And like all things John Wooden, that work started with himself. It took 17 years (not three) for that new field house to be built at UCLA. For every one of those 17 years the task of cleaning the floor fell to him, and he showed no less enthusiasm (the other cornerstone of the Pyramid).

Coach was as clear and consistent in the attitude, actions, and behavior he modeled as he was in his thinking, and he expected his team to follow, especially when it came to those cornerstones. Are you? That's the question you need to ask as you extend your work on your thinking into Lesson Two: How You Set the Example. This lesson challenges you to gain the same clarity and consistency in how you set the example in all that you do: *Do you demonstrate clarity and consistency in the attitude, actions, and behavior you model and expect your team to follow?*

YOUR MOP AND BUCKET ATTITUDE

Cleaning that floor was hardly the extent of Coach's MBA. He worked hard, desperately hard, to set a good example for everyone who either came in direct contact with him or he believed might be influenced indirectly by him. After all he was a teacher at heart. For example, Coach never left a locker room not picked up. He didn't want anyone to be relying on the assistants to pick up after them or think he was asking them to do something he would not do himself. It was entirely possible that, before he picked up the locker room, he had walked into the shower in his suit and tie, picked the soap off the floor, and put it in the dish. He would keep doing that until his players said "Oh!" and did it themselves without asking. He wanted his kids to take pride in where they worked the way he took pride in it. He took as much—more—satisfaction in letters he would get from custodians at other colleges about how incredibly his team behaved as he did in a victory.

Coach attributed his MBA and much of his success to the core values instilled in him by his family. The rules and Seven Point Creed Coach's father, Joshua, shared with his young son had a profound impact on Coach's values and the creation of The Pyramid of Success. (Simple but deep ideas like there is always time for play after the chores and the schoolwork is finished.) But it went beyond that to how they lived and set an example for a young Coach. The Woodens raised their family through the Great Depression. Their behavior, especially in those difficult times, was a model of consistency and demonstrated how values are more caught than taught. As Coach told Lynn, "Dad was a farmer. But when he lost the farm in bankruptcy, he didn't hesitate to humble himself and go to work at the local sanitarium. It was perhaps seen as a lowly occupation, being a bath attendant and a supervisor working continually in hot, humid conditions. He had to demonstrate a servant-like attitude to his team members and his family every single day for 20 years. That example shaped the character of me and my brothers."

When Lynn asked Coach if he felt he was able to live up to his father's creed and the example he set, Coach chuckled softly and answered, "No, but I tried my best, and that was all Dad expected."

When Keith Erickson, a member of Coach's first two NCAA Championship teams and later a Los Angeles Laker, spoke at Coach's memorial service in 2010, he thought about the best thing he could say about his beloved coach and, with tears in his eyes, told the audience: "Coach, your father would be very proud of the man that you have become."

The man he became was the example he set. In creating the course with Coach, Lynn found that the people who knew him best and admired and loved him the most used the following phrases to describe the man and his character:

- ▶ Tried to do the right thing
- ▶ Measured and chose his words carefully
- ▶ Kept his word
- ▶ Reflected true humility
- ▶ Had his priorities straight
- ▶ Refused to be judgmental
- ▶ Lived by the Golden Rule
- ▶ Had an attitude of service

Tried to Do the Right Thing

Whether it was a hard decision he had to make, a heartfelt apology he had to give, or a mistake he had to admit, he always tried to "walk the walk and let his actions speak for themselves." For example, when Coach's 1947 Indiana State team won an invitation to the National Association of Intercollegiate Athletics (NAIA) annual basketball tournament, he turned it down. The NAIA banned Black players, and a player on Coach's team, Clarence Walker, was Black. How are you showing fairness, consideration, and true inclusion when it comes to the people you lead?

_____

_____

_____

_____

Measured and Chose His Words Carefully

For Coach, this statement was all about self-control and making good choices. He never used profanity. He would offer concern but never judgment. He would offer his opinion but never advice unless asked directly for it. He wouldn't speak ill of anyone at any time or place blame. Coach also knew that higher the quality of the listening he was doing, the higher the quality of his words. How carefully are you choosing your words as you communicate with your team and the people you love? Think of a time in which you didn't choose your words as carefully as you could have, your self-control was not as good as it should have been, and you heard those words come back to you from someone in your company or in your family. How did that make you feel? What was the result?

_____

_____

_____

_____

Kept His Word

The University of Minnesota wanted to hire Coach in 1948, and Coach wanted to stay in the Midwest. But when weather prevented Minnesota from calling with an offer, Coach thought there was none in the offing and committed to UCLA. When Minnesota finally reached Coach, he declined the offer as he had given his word to UCLA, and his word was his bond. When was the last time you made a decision in which it was more important to keep your word than to gain any benefit from the decision you made? Have you learned a lesson from going back on your word (breaking a contract or promise or just not doing what you said you would) in order gain a short-term benefit?

_____

_____

_____

_____

Reflected True Humility

If you want to understand how Coach felt about humility, you need only look at the title of a book he often referenced and gave to Lynn: *Humility: True Greatness* by C.J. Mahaney (Multnomah, 2005). Connecting true greatness to humility was a big piece of Coach's goodness-to-greatness search. He believed that God gave grace to the humble. At every point in his career, even during his teams' remarkable championship run, Coach always shared the credit, deflected the praise, shunned the limelight, and started nearly every speech he gave with a self-deprecating story. He loved recalling an article in a small Indiana town newspaper called "Ten Years Ago Today" where they announced that Coach John Wooden was the principal speaker at the annual awards dinner, although "they had hoped to get a prominent person." You don't practice humility. If you have to think about your own humility or how humble you are, you likely aren't too humble. True humility comes from a place of inner peace and strength—and poise. How are you demonstrating this poise?

Had His Priorities Straight

Coach always counseled, "Don't be so busy making a living that you don't have time to make a life." Faith, family and friends, and "hoping He forgives me"—those were what Coach stated his priorities were. He loved teaching basketball but not if there was nothing to teach. The Los Angeles Lakers offered Coach a million dollars a year (30 times what he made at UCLA) and an oceanfront home in La Jolla, California, to join them. He declined. He not only felt there were more important things than basketball and money, but he also felt the players on the Lakers had stopped learning about playing the game of basketball. What are your priorities? Look at your calendar, your checking account, and how you spend your time at home: Are the priorities you think you have reflected in your day-to-day behavior and in how you invest your time and resources?

Refused to Be Judgmental

In a world where we find it so easy to judge others about anything at any time, we need to remember one of the most beautiful phrases of the Bible: "Judge not, that ye be not judged" (Matthew 7:1). It's more important than ever. Coach's dad never let him forget it: "What you put out there, you're gonna get back," Joshua would say. When we're not judging others, we're not likely to be judged ourselves. That refusal to judge was part of the core of Coach taking unpopular positions in order to treat each person with dignity and character regardless of who they were, what their motives might be, or the color of their skin. His support of Black players and coaches helped desegregate sports. Think about the last time you felt unfairly judged. How did it make you feel? Could you have made someone else feel the same way recently based on how you judged them? What was the basis for your judgment?

_____

_____

_____

_____

Lived by the Golden Rule

Coach was a tough, hardworking, demanding disciplinarian who was also kind, interested, considerate, compassionate, and patient. He never put anyone down and always looked for a way to compliment others. He was generous with his time and attention. He treated people the way he wanted to be treated and the way he had seen his parents treat others. Never was that truer than when Purdue University, Coach's alma mater, asked him to be the assistant coach to Mel Taube until Taube's contract expired a few years later. Coach would then take over. He said no. He was loyal to Taube and didn't want to make him a lame-duck coach. How mindful are you of the Golden Rule ("do unto others as you would have them do unto you") in your day-to-day actions? Are you treating people the way you would want to be treated?

_____

_____

_____

_____

Had an Attitude of Service

Countless people have stories about Coach going out of his way to be of service to them with no thought of anything in return. He felt the choice was simple: You could spend your life serving yourself or serving others. Coach's faith and his father's example made the choice clear. Coach believed an attitude of pure service and helping others was essential to true peace of mind. The more you serve others, the more likely you are to move toward that peace of mind. Serving yourself never puts you at peace because you are always in a position of comparing yourself to others and striving not to be outdone by your neighbors' material possessions—the things, Coach said, that never last. Is your life focused more on being served or serving others?

_____

_____

_____

_____

THE WISDOM OF WOODEN • THE WISDOM OF WOODEN • THE WISDOM OF WOODEN

STAND FIRM IN YOUR BELIEFS

Coach had a list of expectations that he gave to every team at the start of the season. They didn't change a lot from 1948 to 1975, which made it notable when they did. One such case was the dress code. Until Bill Walton joined the team in 1971, Coach required his players to travel clean shaven and in blazers and ties. Walton noted that even the administration now dressed in turtlenecks and jeans and asked Coach why they had to be so formal. Coach told Walton he was right and changed his rules to only require players to be neat and clean-shaven to get on the bus. Walton, the reigning NCAA Player of the Year, then decided to challenge the second part of that new dress code:

He showed up for picture day and the first practice of the season sporting a full beard, not having shaved since the end of last season. Coach told him to shave it off. Walton insisted he had the right to have facial hair. "That's correct, Bill. You do have that right," Coach replied, adding that he also did not have the right to make Walton shave it. But, Coach continued, "I do have the right to say who is going to play on my team, and we're going to miss you." Walton got cleaned up in a hurry.

THE WOODEN WAY WORKsheet

Your Mop and Bucket Attitude

Preparation, time put in, level of intensity . . . John Wooden was always the hardest worker on the team from the practices he ran to his Mop and Bucket Attitude about cleaning the floor of the "B.O. Barn." He knew all of it mattered for the example he set. What would people say about you and the example you set?

Who is at the top of the list of the people you set the example for in life (your family, team, community . . .)? Who is watching you today?

_____

_____

_____

_____

THE WOODEN WAY WORKsheet

Assess your recent behavior, engagement, and involvement with those people. How have you set a good example for them?

_____

_____

_____

_____

_____

Was there anything you did or said that did not set a good example? Why?

_____

_____

_____

_____

_____

Reach out to three people on the list whose opinion and candor you respect and ask them the same questions you just asked yourself. How do the two lists match up? How can you bridge any gaps?

_____

_____

_____

_____

_____

SOMEONE IS ALWAYS WATCHING YOU

Coach's son Jim said this about his father: "Dad talked about what he believed. He followed it. And he never stopped thinking about ways to make small improvements. He was always teaching, but he was also always thinking and learning." Thinking about how you set the example and actually living and consistently re-evaluating that example are where too many leaders and companies fall off the Pyramid. And you can only expect your people to follow what they see you doing.

Jason understood that at GoldenComm long before he met Lynn, particularly when it came to recognizing service to the company. Twice a year, the company has bonfires when everyone gets together and Jason does what he calls "affirmations." He knows a lot of people never get recognized, or "affirmed," by their leaders or company. So, at the bonfires, Jason calls up everyone who is celebrating a work anniversary and affirms them one at a time. He tells a story about how they met, what he has seen in their work in the past, and what he sees today. He goes back as far as his notes from their first interviews and takes great care to be specific. Then, having set that example, he asks the company to add to the affirmation: After they are done, Jason ices the cake and counts out $100 bills in their palms, one for each year of service.

That being said, it works the other way at GoldenComm too. Not everyone is a fit; Jason works hard to set the example when he is moving people out as well as up or affirming them. "Everyone at GoldenComm knows that I've only fired one person in the history of the company—for stealing. Most people who leave us do so for more money than we can pay or because they can't afford the cost of living in California. I will do all I can to help those people, and that's part of the reason we started a Utah office. But for the people who have not performed well according to their peer reviews and get average results? That means they are not a good fit for us. For them, we have a private process in which I work with them on their resumes, interviewing skills, and prospecting. I make 30 percent of their job finding a job. After all, if they are good enough for me to hire, then they should be good for someone else. At the end of each week, they have to show me what that 30 percent looked like. I work with them until they find something, because I don't believe it's easy to find a job if you don't have one. Inevitably they all get jobs. Have I heard a lot of criticism about this process over the years? Of course. Ironically, my greatest critic turned out to be a beneficiary. He stopped being a good fit, so I helped him find a better one. Suddenly, he didn't think it was such a bad idea."

But Jason also takes responsibility and holds himself and the company responsible for the people who don't make it: "If someone fails, that means we didn't do a good job of articulating our expectations, what it is like to work here, and what makes people here successful. If we had done a better job, we wouldn't be in that place. I'm the leader, and I'm saying that. That's an example I have to set. I own the mistakes. I don't say 'You stink at your job. You sold us on something you're not.' That's not how we work. The example we are showing is consideration. It's not personal. It has nothing to do with how much I like you. It's about helping others and putting consideration of others above any personal feelings. Everyone is a member of the GoldenComm family, and I'm not going to leave family on the streets."

Jason knows GoldenComm is only as good as its processes and the day-to-day behavior of its people. When he needed a better foundation for the day-to-day behavior of the company and the values that guided that behavior, he turned to Lynn and Coach—and brought his team into the discussion. If Jason thought of his people as family, then he had to bring that family into the discussion of the values they would share. It couldn't be him asking "What messages did I send?" and "What does my team need to get, see, and understand that they are not getting from my current example?" It had to be "What messages are *we* sending?" and "What do *we* need to get, see, and understand?"

How do we know and live our vision and priorities—and are they what we want them to be for ourselves and others?

Lynn showed Jason's team at GoldenComm how the Pyramid drives success, compels you to ask how you are setting the example for each one of its blocks, and provided the foundation for GoldenComm to build its values on. But a "value"—defined as a principle, standard, or quality considered worthwhile or of high "net worth"—only means something if Jason as CEO invested his time, thought, and effort to show the importance of those values in the way GoldenComm operated. So, he did. For example:

- The core values of GoldenComm based on The Pyramid of Success—hard work, business acumen, technical ability, service, grit, and transparency—became the core of the evaluation process for all employees, including Jason.

- To start every week, Jason now sends a TGIM (Thank God, It's Monday) email to the entire staff with quick-hit content that aims to provide everyone with a head start to the week tied to the core values and the Pyramid. Its purpose is to give things to think about that will encourage everyone to consider the quality of their thinking and the example they are setting.

- He integrated the blocks of the Pyramid into part of the homework he gives every prospective employee after he interviews them. He asks every candidate to send him an email the following day on which block resonated with them and why in three sentences or less. "About 40 percent do the work and follow the directions," says Jason. "They are the ones who have the potential to work and succeed at the company."

From those affirmations to the Monday emails to much more (such as monthly "lunch and learn" events and a learning library stocked with multiple copies of free books Jason loves), Jason knows he can never stop watching what he is doing because someone is always watching what he is doing and following his lead. Always remember to say to yourself "I'm a coach, and I must set a good example every day."

THE WOODEN WAY WORKsheet

Someone Is Always Watching You

We can't tell you how you can best set the example in your professional and personal life, but you can use The Pyramid of Success for your template. Go to the foundation of the Pyramid and ask how you are setting the example in all five blocks. Be specific. Look

THE WOODEN WAY WORKsheet

back to your assessment: How could you do better than you are doing now?

Industriousness: Do your people see you doing the things that really matter and not wasting your time on things that are not worth doing?

_____

_____

_____

Friendship: Do others feel the friendship that you're offering? Do they feel that they have a friend in you who they can rely on?

_____

_____

_____

Loyalty: Do your team members know where your loyalties lie—the people and things you value most and your sense of loyalty for the business?

_____

_____

_____

Cooperation: Are you modeling every day the best way to do things, not your own way of doing things? Does that come

THE WOODEN WAY WORKsheet

across when difficult decisions need to be made and resilience is required?

_____

_____

_____

Enthusiasm: Are you showing every day what you're excited about, and are you excited about the things that matter most? Is your team catching your enthusiasm?

_____

_____

_____

WHO IS FOLLOWING YOU?

For more than 60 years, John Wooden kept a picture of a father and son walking down the beach on his desk. The father was dressed as a ship's captain with white cap, white duck pants, and white deck shoes. The young boy, also wearing a white captain's hat, walked a few paces behind, seemingly walking in his father's footsteps. To the left of the picture was a framed copy of a poem he received in 1936 shortly after his son Jim was born called "A Little Fellow Follows Me."

A Little Fellow Follows Me

A careful man I want to be,
A little fellow follows me;
I do not dare to go astray,
For fear he'll go the self-same way.
I cannot once escape his eyes,

Whate'er he sees me do, he tries;
Like me he says he's going to be,
The little chap who follows me.
He thinks that I'm so very fine,
Believes in every word of mine;
The base in me he must not see,
The little chap who follows me.
I must remember as I go,
Through summer's sun and winter's snow;
I'm building for the years to be,
The little chap who follows me.

Every day he sat at his desk, the picture and the poem reminded Coach of his responsibility and opportunity to set an example. He shared the poem every time he spoke in public, be it basketball campers and parents, coaches, the military, or CEOs. Lynn was so moved when he saw the picture and poem, he created a personal version of it (see Figure 8–1) with images of the Guerin men: his oldest son, youngest son, and grandchildren.

FIGURE 8–1 *Lynn's "A Little Fellow Follows Me"*

Who and what reminds you of your opportunity and responsibility to set a good example every day?

THE WOODEN WAY WORKsheet

Who Is Following You?

Who is following you?

_____

What is your relationship to them?

_____

What is your responsibility to them?

_____

_____

_____

_____

Why are these relationships important to you?

_____

_____

_____

_____

_____

_____

_____

THE WOODEN WAY WORKsheet

Now think of an image or item that can serve as a reminder to you of this relationship. What would it be? Do you have your own poem, song, or phrase that reminds you of this person? Write it out and use it to create something. Place it somewhere you can see it every day and never forget the importance of the example you must set for your family, team, and all the most important people in your life—everyone else you may have the privilege to teach, coach, mentor, influence, and serve.

"Everyone is a teacher to someone;
maybe it's your children, maybe it's
your neighbor, maybe it is someone
under your supervision in some
other way, and in one way
or another you are teaching
them by your actions."

CHAPTER 9

Lesson Three:
How You Teach

W
hen leaders ask themselves "How am I doing?" the answer lies in asking and answering another question: How are the people that I am leading, coaching, and teaching doing? That's the question the leader of a team of law enforcement agents was asking when he engaged Lynn to assess his team against The Pyramid of Success. After taking the team assessment, the leader was stunned by the results. The biggest gaps between perception and reality and the lowest behavior scores were on the Foundation (industriousness and loyalty) and the Strength of the Human Character side of the Mortar (sincerity and honesty)—all among the behaviors the agents said they valued most. Lynn quickly got down to the answers as to why: The team felt misinformed and misled by people in the organization. Information was being kept from them and trust among team members had eroded. As they discussed the assessment, Lynn recognized a problem in this group of public servants that he saw in so many offices: They had bosses, but no one was teaching them.

Do you embrace the role of teaching in your organization as a CEO or leader? John Wooden believed the most important responsibility of coaches and leaders, when it came to the actual playing of the game, was to teach their players properly and effectively to execute the various fundamentals of the "game." But Coach also wanted those under his supervision to be motivated—to strive to be their best because he believed in them rather than from any fear of punishment. His love, loyalty, and support for all his players throughout their lifetime and his was a model for the ages and what he believed was the essence and opportunity of being a coach and teacher. Do your people have that? Are they learning from you to develop, improve, and consistently perform at a high level? Those are the questions at the heart of Lesson Three: How You Teach: *Teach by setting the example and using preparation, effort, methodology, and commitment to create healthy habits that instinctively produce excellence under ever increasing pressure.*

In this lesson, you'll consider your readiness to be a teacher and consider Coach's teaching techniques to develop and improve your own.

YOUR READINESS TO TEACH

What does it mean to be ready to be a teacher? It starts with a joy of learning, not just leading—and not just having others learn from you. Coaches and leaders are learners. They have the confidence to admit they don't know what they don't know and keep working on it.

Coach maintained a deep intellectual curiosity and a great capacity for absorbing, organizing, and remembering large amounts of information. He was a voracious reader and an enthusiastic lifelong learner with extraordinary mental and physical discipline. He was a creative big-picture visionary who could imagine, see, and describe all that was possible. He could then break those concepts down to their components and create lessons around them that produced high performance. Finally, he provided the inspiration for giving maximum effort and ultimate achievement. All those things contributed to Coach being way ahead of his time in using teaching and learning as the foundation of his leadership, coaching, and success model. What he did to rewrite the standards of team accomplishment have found their way into the game plans of corporate leaders, educators, business owners, and the homes of American families.

Jason was doing some of that and looking for more when he engaged Lynn to help him be the best he could be so that his team at GoldenComm could be the best they could be. As Jason broke away from the "Jason Way" that defined GoldenComm—the core values and proprietary platforms he put in place—and moved to shared values and platforms, he allowed his team to execute at a higher level and become self-sufficient and employable. He also set up a more shared system for learning, using the Pyramid and integrating it into how the company worked.

To be clear, Jason had been a teacher (in his various roles as a corporate trainer) and had seen himself in the role of teacher at GoldenComm before he met Lynn, but he recognized his limitations on what he could and could not teach. "I teach all the time. I'm just not teaching code. There isn't a twentysomething that I would hire who could ever be taught coding or technical things by me," says Jason. "I'm the expert on my company's behavior. I teach that. I often describe our company as one comprised of sophisticated Lego-ists. You can make some incredible sculptures if you have the right pieces. I help those pieces work together and get better, and we keep building new sculptures."

A teacher is not always the smartest in the room or the most skilled—and may never have been in his career. Skill is only one block on The Pyramid of Success, which explains why the greatest coaches of all time in sports were almost never the best hitters, tacklers, shooters, skaters, or runners. The greatest coaches were ready to work on the other 24 blocks of the Pyramid and turn the people who had those skills into winning teams with healthy habits. They leveraged those skills and others' expertise, welcoming every person and everything that could be helpful to them. They had boundless enthusiasm for the hard work. And they always—*always*—understood the value of learning in these lessons—how they thought, set the example, taught, led, and mentored.

Teaching and learning are at the center of those lessons. That's why learning is everywhere at GoldenComm, from the learning library filled with free books to the monthly lunch-and-learns (21 minutes of presentation on any topic, 21 minutes of Q&A, and 21 minutes of lunch). The company is also working to extend the Pyramid into the lessons learned from the projects they complete. This goes beyond the usual facts, figures, and feedback on what went well and what needed improvement. The lessons learned include a team survey designed with Lynn that looks like the Wooden Course assessment. Everyone evaluates the project and their work according to ten blocks from the Pyramid the company feels are essential to any project's success: Industriousness, Cooperation, Enthusiasm, Alertness, Initiative, Intentness, Skill, Confidence, Team Spirit, and Competitive Greatness. Finally, they assess themselves on one statement: I achieved success according to John Wooden's definition.

"Coach would look at industriousness and ask, 'How hard we did we work *and* did we do and work on the right things?'" says Jason. "Coach knew you can't confuse activity with achievement. The Pyramid allows us to ask the right questions in the right ways to learn and get better: How well did the team come together and listen to each other and respond appropriately? Were we into the work? Did we pick up good client signals and have a good relationship with them? Did we see when things were going wrong? Anticipate mistakes? Adapt our behavior? Feel confident doing the work? Fight through it all? Were there any skill sets we needed that we didn't have? Industriousness and alertness were the low scores on a disastrous project—what could we have done better. These are valuable teaching lessons."

But learning like this is valued at a company only if it is valued by the leader, something Jason believes in deeply and extends to all parts of the company. "When I brought in a new HR manager, I role-played with her on how to make HR more effective and how HR could be fun," Jason says. "She came in thinking HR was about compliance. No. HR here is about everyone learning rapidly. We don't have anyone complaining about the work environment. We have unmetered sick and vacation time. I ask people all the time if they have the tools to do their jobs. We give them ongoing peer reviews. Yes, I want my HR person to make sure we comply with all the government rules and regulations. But HR is mostly about employee development to me. It's about using the Pyramid, living our core values, and helping us teach and get better at what we do. It's not easy. It never stops. But it's rewarding."

Coach would understand all what Jason said, especially that the work never stopped. That was the only way, as a teacher rather than just a coach, to always look for ways to improve himself and those around him. Are you ready to work on that?

THE WISDOM OF WOODEN • THE WISDOM OF WOODEN • THE WISDOM OF WOODEN

CONTINUAL LEARNING UNDER ANY CIRCUMSTANCE

Kareem Abdul-Jabbar's sophomore season was something to behold. In his first game in 1967, he scored 56 points, breaking the UCLA single-game record. He then led the team to a 29-1 record and the NCAA Championship (the only loss going to Houston when Abdul-Jabbar was sidelined with an eye injury). Abdul-Jabbar was named NCAA Player of the Year.

The following season, the NCAA outlawed dunking, saying the shot lacked skill and citing injury concerns. The rules committee never mentioned Lew Alcindor, as Abdul-Jabbar was then known (he converted to Islam in 1968 but did not start using his Muslim name until 1971), but the move was widely nicknamed the "Lew Alcindor Rule." Abdul-Jabbar, who regularly dunked on opponents, believed the shot was outlawed because of him too. Coach told Abdul-Jabbar, it made no difference. "I told him this was going to make him better," Coach told Lynn. "I told him he was going to have to become a much better player and more fully develop his game with different shots. Ultimately it was going to help him."

And Coach was ready to help. He worked with Abdul-Jabbar not only on his trademark skyhook but also on a variety of shots, as well as his team skills. The result? Abdul-Jabbar led UCLA to two more championships before he went on to become (and remains) the greatest scorer in NBA history. He is widely considered the best center to ever play the game.

THE WOODEN WAY WORKsheet

Your Readiness to Teach

Are you prepared for the role of "teacher" in your day-to-day work, home, and family life? Following is a readiness exercise for a coach and leader who must also be a teacher.

Am I comfortable and confident in the role of teacher—why or why not?

_____

_____

_____

_____

Is my confidence justified based on how I see my readiness to teach? If not, how can I prepare?

_____

_____

_____

_____

Who is my target group of "students"?

_____

_____

_____

_____

THE WOODEN WAY WORKsheet

Can I identify the areas where my teaching could have a significant impact with them?

_____

_____

_____

_____

Do you have a person who can help you become the quality of teacher you need and want to be? Who is it? How can they help you move forward in your teaching role?

_____

_____

_____

_____

COACH'S TEACHING TECHNIQUES

As we move forward into leading and mentoring, you are probably noticing how intertwined Coach's lessons are with themselves, not just the Pyramid. That is by design, especially when it comes to how you teach, which of course was what the Pyramid was designed for: to help Coach be a better teacher. The construction of that Pyramid also reflected Coach's love for civil engineering, which is what he originally went to college to study. He had thoughts of building roads and bridges. He saw in his head how their parts would fit together and help people get to their destinations. Ultimately, Coach decided to build a different kind of bridge to teach people to cross and get where they were going successfully, and that work as a teacher required as much (if not more) capability and effort.

As a teacher, Coach understood human capacity and the opportunity to truly be your best and give your total effort. What did he do as a coach and teacher to bring out the best in individuals and teams, and inspire them to go beyond what they thought they could accomplish? How did he create a dynamic teaching and learning process where the striving for perfection produced extraordinary results? He followed these nine teaching techniques.

Be an Expert

No one studied the topics of basketball and life more than Coach, and he remained a student of each until the day he died. He never let success on the scoreboard interfere with those pursuits. Every summer throughout his career he did a research project on one aspect of the game where he believed he and the team needed to improve, like rebounding (assume every shot will be missed and find the place where the ball is going to be, which helped even the shorter players get to the ball first), free-throw shooting (asking coaches whose teams were good at free throws how they worked on them), and defensive strategy (he felt the best defenses—individual and team—won championships, especially pressure defenses). He never let his ego interfere either: As much as others reached out to him, he constantly consulted with other coaches and performance experts who could provide knowledge and understanding he felt he lacked.

Be Direct and Precise in Your Explanations

Coach was so exceptional at this technique, he was the subject of an academic study. In a 2004 issue of *The Sport Psychologist*, Ronald Gallimore (UCLA) and Roland Tharp (University of California, Santa Cruz) published a revisitation of their 1976 case study of Coach when both were at UCLA: "What a Coach Can Teach a Teacher, 1975–2004: Reflections and Reanalysis of John Wooden's Teaching Practices." They observed and analyzed Coach's afternoon practices for content, time, and direct communication with his team, and they recorded 2,326 teaching or instructional acts from Coach during 30 hours of practice. In fact, more than 75 percent of all his communication was instructional. Yet Coach never spoke for more than 20 seconds, and his demonstrations took no more than five seconds. Think about that when you are preparing your next PowerPoint.

Be Highly Organized

Gallimore and Tharp found that Coach's practices were "exact and unvarying" in order to fit into his precise schedule. Individual work began at 3 P.M., and team practice ran from 3:29 to 5:29 P.M. No one dared to be late—ever. Prior to that, Coach spent two hours every day with his assistants planning those practices. Each practice was recorded, tracked, and analyzed to see where improvements could be made. Constant activity, high intensity, and work on the soundness of the players' fundamentals were directed to produce correct habits and skill improvements.

Teach by Example

Teaching by example was not just about values but demonstration. Coach was always on the floor with the team. Even in his final years as a coach, he could demonstrate proper footwork and balance. When Coach saw something not being done correctly, he would stop the action and follow a three-step process:

- ► Demonstrate the right way to do it.
- ► Demonstrate what the player or team was doing wrong.
- ► Demonstrate the right way to do it *again*.

To eliminate repetitive mistakes, he was patient with progress and maintained self-control when his team did not correct those mistakes quickly. He was never in too big a hurry or too caught up in achieving immediate results to the point that he was unwilling to do something the right way.

Teach by Repetition

Coach followed what he had been taught as the four laws of learning: explanation, demonstration, imitation, and repetition. As you might have guessed from the previous technique, Coach placed extra weight on repetition to create a correct habit that could be produced under pressure.

To ensure that goal was achieved, he took those laws and expanded them to eight: explanation, demonstration, imitation, repetition, repetition, repetition, repetition, and repetition.

Plan for the Individual and the Team

"You can't improve the team if you don't improve each player," Coach told Lynn. "You have to know them to be able to do that, not just their skills but how they think and what gets the response you are looking for." Coach always knew where and how his players needed to improve, and he and his assistants were always ready with a plan and capable of teaching what was needed for that improvement on the individual and team level. He tracked his players' practice routines over their careers to see where ongoing and new improvement in skill and the development was needed. This allowed him to anticipate mistakes before they happened.

Create a Positive and Disciplined Environment

Coach understood the difference between discipline and punishment. Punishment creates antagonism, and it's hard to get positive results when you antagonize. Discipline is about learning and improvement through correction and repetition. Those corrections should never be personal or degrading in any way, and new information should be aimed at the act, never the actor. That's what makes an environment positive, not praise (especially when it isn't warranted). Gallimore and Tharp found double the amount of corrections to praise and encouragement in Coach's practices (14 percent compared to 7 percent). The key was to focus on the information that can be used to improve a specific situation, not the person. His persistence was matched only by his patience when it came to managing expectations.

Break Complex Issues into Simpler Details

Coach explained his teaching process and approach this way to Lynn: "The greatest holiday feast is eaten one bite at a time. Gulp it down all at once and you get indigestion. I discovered the same is true in teaching. Teach what you want and need to do best one simple step at a time. Little things done well are probably the greatest secret to success. If you do enough small things right, big things can happen." Did this desire for simplicity make Coach's teams predictable? Sometimes. But knowing what Coach would do and stopping it were two different things—and you had to execute better and outlast his team's condition.

Teach More Than Your Game

Coach had a teachable view on success: Success in coaching and in life should not be based on the number of games won or lost or points scored. True success in the game should be based on how close individuals came to giving their maximum effort and performing at their highest level of capability. Remember: True success can be attained only through self-satisfaction in knowing that you did everything within the limits of your ability to become the best you are capable of becoming. To Coach, character was the foundation of individual success, a successful team, and a successful life. Persons with good character were the kind of people Coach believed made better teammates and a stronger team. Coach believed it was his job to model good character every day, in every situation.

Coach learned, deeply believed, and practiced these teaching techniques, which he believed were the heart of all coaching and leadership. He often said he was just a teacher of the game of life and the sport of basketball. His success in both demonstrates the critical importance that teaching has in the success of a leader and the coach. He knew what needed to be taught to each player, position, and the team as a whole; how much time he would spend on each of them; and how he would get his point of view across. But one point of view mattered most: learning to understand between right and wrong and acquiring the sense and maturity to make right choices as you work to achieve true success.

THE WOODEN WAY WORKsheet

Teaching Techniques and Potential Success as a Teacher

Using the following criteria, evaluate potential success for your *next* important teaching opportunity to better prepare in areas you think you might fall short.

THE WOODEN WAY WORKsheet

1. I have the knowledge, experience, expertise, and credibility to teach in this area.

2. I have a powerful teachable point of view on the most important fundamentals that need to be taught.

3. I can teach what I need to quickly and clearly, being precise and direct, and not using more time than needed.

4. I can use my experience to teach by example—what to do, why to do it, and how to do it.

5. I see opportunities where repetition can be used powerfully.

6. I am able to break down complex issues into smaller, simpler details and tasks.

7. I can create and maintain a positive environment.

8. I can see opportunities for adding value that help team members be better people, not just more productive and get results.

Following the opportunity, go back and re-evaluate your assessment of your potential. Where did you equal and exceed your expectations, and where did you fall short? Why? What can you do to improve? Talk to your team and use their feedback and The Pyramid of Success as your guides.

_____

_____

_____

_____

_____

*"I consider leadership
a sacred trust: helping to
mold character and instill
productive principles
and values."*

CHAPTER 10

Lesson Four:
How You Lead

The first thing Lynn did with Jason and his leadership team was have them take the Wooden Course team assessment—and Jason was excited to read the results. Lynn had told him most companies followed a similar pattern: The team recorded their highest scores when assessing themselves, the next highest scores when assessing their teammates and the company as a whole, and their lowest scores when assessing the CEO and leadership. Meanwhile, the leaders at those companies scored themselves highest and their people lowest. But in the best-run companies, Lynn said, the pattern was reversed: The leaders scored themselves lower than their teammates, and the team scored the leaders highest and themselves lowest.

"Exceptional employees and exceptional leaders both rank themselves below others on the Pyramid's behaviors," Lynn said to Jason. "The best always realize they have more to learn, and the worst always think they are better than they are."

Jason was not surprised: "That is how it should be. If your peers are saying you're doing better than you say you're doing, you're killing it. Poorly run companies have people who say everyone is stupid but me."

What *was* surprising to Jason? He was not killing it as a leader. Looking over the results was sobering: His employees were telling him that they were outperforming him. "That was a bruiser," he said. "I hired Lynn to be a leadership coach, because I couldn't wait to see what a good leader I was. I thought we had good things going, and I wanted to make things better. I wanted an affirmation. And my report card was a B-minus."

What GoldenComm's team assessments and Lynn helped Jason see was how eye-opening these lessons can be as they progress—even for a leader and company like GoldenComm that was doing well by most measures. Turnover was low, revenue was growing, and money was being made. GoldenComm was delivering on their promise to make websites work harder. Clients were happy. Creativity and collaboration were strong. They were hiring. The assessments echoed all those things as well as the fact that Jason was doing great when it came to how he thought and set the example. His teaching was also solid. Yet according to his team, when it came to leadership and mentoring the Wooden Way, Jason was falling short.

What Jason needed to do was use the principles and guidance the Pyramid provided to improve his leadership and earn the level of respect and trust of the people he was leading and serving. That's a big part of Lesson Four: How You Lead: *Encouraging individuals to work together for the common good and the best possible results, while at the same time letting them know they did it themselves.* In this lesson, you will assess your own leadership against Coach's definition, understand how you define it, and assess yourself against Coach's leadership fundamentals so you can better serve others in your own work and life.

DEFINING LEADERSHIP

The short description of this lesson was actually based on Coach's simple, yet powerful, definition of leadership: "The ability to get individuals to work together for the common good and the best possible results, while at the same time letting them know they did it themselves." To Coach, achieving that level of leadership required four components from a coach:

1. Fostering cooperation
2. Defining the vision, mission, and goals
3. Setting performance standards and expectations
4. Providing motivation and encouragement

To be clear, the assessments Jason received did not show him *failing* Coach's definition of leadership or any of its four components. Jason was not a coach with a losing record who needed to take some drastic action to turn things around. But he also wasn't Coach in the last years of his career—building a dynasty and leading UCLA to ten championships in 12 years. Like many successful leaders, Jason was like Coach in the decades before he won his first championship: winning but still not quite reaching the level of competitive greatness on the scoreboard or in life—not quite able to create that sustained level of excellence and championship behavior in his team culture and keeping it there. Jason needed to keep working on his leadership, and the team assessments quantified the Pyramid's skills and behaviors that he was excelling at and those he fell short on in the eyes of his team. The gaps were enlightening: Confidence, enthusiasm, honesty, integrity, and faith were high on both Jason and the team's assessments while patience, self-control, fight, and loyalty were much lower on the team's scores. The lowest scores on individual questions noted a lack of genuine friendships, the fact that priorities were not clear, and the absence of a clear accountability system and regular monitoring behavior and performance.

"It was brutal," Jason recalls.

But instead of just discussing the results, Jason and the team worked— *together*—satisfying Coach's first component to achieving leadership success (cooperation): Making sure everyone is more interested in finding the best way to do things than in having their own way. They then worked with Lynn to break down the Pyramid's foundations, fundamentals, and behaviors into GoldenComm's six core values (service, business acumen, grit, technical ability, transparency, and hard work), which were based on the Pyramid, thus addressing the second component (defining the mission).

To address the third component of standards and expectations, GoldenComm's entire performance evaluation system was rebuilt around the six core values, with any pay increase based on these reviews. The system is highly collaborative and peer driven. Employees pick three people they think would be good evaluators of their work. GoldenComm promises it will use at least two of those people in their evaluations out of a total of four. Questions are scored on a 1 to 5 scale. The goal is to have the employee's and the evaluators' scores on each of the six values average within 0.5 of each other. Anything more and the evaluators and the employee did not see themselves the same way, and there was a disconnect not only on the performance but on how the core values were being lived by the employees and perceived by their peers.

"The hope is always that employees will rank themselves the same or lower than their peers; no one can think they are better than everyone else," Jason says. "When they do, that's usually an employee I need to coach out, not up."

The impact the core values had on the team's work and connecting those values to the performance evaluation system was powerful and self-motivating for the team, realizing Coach's final component: motivation and encouragement. The effect was that widespread socialization was no longer reserved to the company Christmas party: Employees began to move around the company more freely, initiating conversations with everyone. "Loyalty, friendship, cooperation, team spirit, enthusiasm, poise, being yourself . . . all those things are coached into the group, yet they are doing it themselves," adds Jason. "It became a place to be aspirational, inspirational, to take risks, to act with the boundary-less behavior I wanted but still focused on the intent of my company. It *was* a sobering lesson, but I learned what the Pyramid can do to define leadership at my company that was already doing well and worked to develop the fundamentals of leadership that Coach expected of himself. And I need to keep working on them."

COACH'S LEADERSHIP LESSONS

Long before Lynn met Coach and Jason met Lynn, they had already been in positions of leadership and had done well, thanks to the leaders they learned from. Who taught and shaped your leadership lessons? Coach's earliest leadership lessons came from his father and his three basketball coaches: Earl Warriner, Glenn Curtis, and Ward Lambert.

Earl Warriner was Coach's grade school coach and first mentor. Coach often told the story of how Warriner once refused to play Coach (the star of the team), because he forgot his uniform. He kept him out even as the team was getting beat. Warriner taught Coach the first of four leadership lessons that night—lessons that stayed with Coach for a lifetime:

- ► There are no stars or privileged individuals on any team.
- ► You can never compromise principles for the sake of convenience.
- ► You must recognize and respect the right of every individual to differ in their opinions on issues that matter to them.
- ► When you are wrong, you have to demonstrate that you are mature enough to always admit it without rationalization, alibi, or excuse.

Coach had a more complicated relationship with his high school Coach Glenn Curtis, whose team he quit for two weeks during his sophomore season over a dispute and residual bad feelings about what Coach believed was unfair treatment his brother Cat had received a year earlier. But Curtis still passed on important lessons regarding skills and discipline, as well as the challenge and importance of getting individuals to come together as a team, the goal of getting that team to rise to its uppermost levels of effort and competency, and the importance of keeping players from becoming emotional on the court.

But the most important and influential coach in Coach's development as a person, athlete, and coach was Ward "Piggy" Lambert, the coach at Purdue. When Coach arrived at the school, he saw a need for direction and advice. He gave Coach confidence on and off the court, which helped shape his coaching process and principles, including:

▶ A coach's primary function is to not make better players but to make better people.

▶ A coach's primary vision must be focused not on seeing limitations but on seeing possibilities.

▶ The primary components of a strong team are conditioning, skill, team spirit, unity, and cohesion.

▶ The level of performance you see as a coach will likely be equal to the level of confidence you instill in the player.

▶ Caring, compassion, and communication are keys to building productive relationships and high performance.

▶ Coaches are most responsible for teaching good habits shared through experience, values, and wisdom—telling people what they need to hear, not what they want to hear.

Every one of these leadership lessons from these coaches are reflected in The Pyramid of Success and Coach's leadership elements.

THE WOODEN WAY WORKsheet

Defining Leadership

Coach's definition of leadership ("the ability to get individuals to work together for the common good and the best possible results,

THE WOODEN WAY WORKsheet

while at the same time letting them know they did it themselves")
was immensely teachable, as were the components he broke that
definition into (fostering cooperation, defining the vision/mission
goals, setting performance standards/expectations, providing
motivation and encouragement). Are yours?

How do you define leadership? With Coach's definition and components in mind (and thinking about the people who shaped your
leadership for the better), develop your own definition of leadership.

_____

_____

_____

What are the principle tasks you will have to accomplish to model
that definition?

_____

_____

_____

Look at the four components Coach believed you must have to
achieve leadership success. What are your components?

_____

_____

_____

_____

LEADERSHIP ELEMENTS OF A COACH

You must never forget that to be an excellent coach you must be a leader and not merely a person with authority. Your influence is a sacred trust. You are in a position to help shape and mold the character of individuals, teams, and entire organizations. People will look to you for guidance in relationships and all aspects of business and life. Serving those people, seeing through their eyes, and having faith they can achieve the goals you have set are the traits of a true leader.

Everyone has the potential to become this coach and leader if they understand the fundamentals of getting individuals to work together. These fundamentals can be learned, and Coach held a clear view of what they were and the capabilities coaches need to help their teams reach their full potential and achieve success:

- Earn respect and trust
- Be just and fair
- Be ready and willing to risk everything
- Bring out the best in people
- Express total commitment
- Set the direction or goal
- Study human nature
- Take responsibility
- Practice love and balance

Let's explore each of these in more detail.

Earn Respect and Trust

Coach felt it was essential for leaders to have the respect and trust of those under their supervision. You need to show faith in your people—to believe in and trust them to draw out the best in them and to earn that trust in you. Coach considered leadership a sacred trust: "helping to mold character and instill productive principles and values." That trust was earned as was the respect that went with it. To earn that respect, you must first give it, starting by clearly communicating to the people you supervise that they are working *with* you, not *for* you. You need to say "Let's go!" rather than "Get going!" If you show respect for your team, they will do what you ask and more. There is no clock-watching, obligatory work, or drudgery when a coach has that respect.

Be Just and Fair

A coach's most powerful ally is his or her own example, especially when it comes to fairness. Coach defined fairness as "giving all people the treatment they earn and deserve." That, Coach said, "doesn't mean treating everyone alike. That's unfair, because everyone does not earn the same treatment." Being fair in this manner simply requires you to root out any partiality you may be showing. You may never be completely fair, but when you make the sincere effort to do so, you will further earn the trust and respect of your people, as well as their understanding. This effort will create positive attitudes that will resonate and multiply within your team and office and extend into all parts of your life.

Be Ready and Willing to Risk Everything

Sometimes there are people in our organizations who we assume are star players because we love the short-term results they're producing. Perhaps you have a superstar salesperson who treats others badly but is ultimately counterproductive long term for the culture and the team you are trying to build. Perhaps you have a manager who gets results from his team, which makes you happy, but doesn't treat the people on that team very well, which makes you unhappy. Being ready and willing to risk everything means being willing to fire people like that. The star of your team is the team, and those kinds of "results stars" are not team players when it comes to anything beyond numbers on the scoreboard. Nothing comes before the team's integrity and importance. Coach had a clear idea of what he wanted to do and little tolerance for those individuals who resisted his concepts. When Coach was pushed, like when Bill Walton showed up in that full beard, his beliefs came first. He was willing to let the best player in college basketball go. But it wasn't all risk. While it may seem foolish to some that Coach went to those lengths for what he believed, he was not without a backup plan. Walton was a star player, but Coach had future NBA first-rounder, Swen Nater, ready to go.

Bring Out the Best in People

When Lynn asked Coach if he guided his family the same way he guided his teams, Coach responded, "No, I guided my team pretty much like I guided my family with respect, appreciation, gentle discipline, and love." Every single member of your team needs to feel wanted, respected, and appreciated. Pride is used as a better motivator than fear, especially to produce long-term results. Praise your "behind the scenes" players publicly and let your star players receive their praise from the public. But remember that the "star" of any team is the team, and the "coach" is someone who can give correction without causing resentment. As Jason likes to say, "No one shows up to work and says 'I want to suck today' or 'My goal is to go to work today and be really average—mediocre.' Yet that's what will happen if you don't take steps to take risks and get better. That is the culture and the expectations and the environment that you set."

Express Total Commitment

Coach Wooden was committed to:

- ▶ his faith, family, and friends.
- ▶ his integrity.
- ▶ his definition and Pyramid of Success.
- ▶ his teams and their development, personally and on the court.
- ▶ his relentless pursuit of daily, incremental improvement.
- ▶ his standards for meeting daily expectations.

What are you committed to on a day-to-day basis? Is it the vision and mission of the company? Is it the care and consideration for your customers and clients? Your people? Or is it the scoreboard, the monthly results, the profit and loss statement, the balance sheet, and the stock price above all else? Your goal is to lead the team into success by being the most enthusiastic and encouraging member of the team and total commitment to everything that you do.

Set the Direction or Goal

A team without a coach and leader is like a ship without a rudder; it will never get to its destination because it has no control over where it is going.

You must make certain that the team is clear on the destination—and that the destination is something totally controllable and reachable if the team performs at its best. This means you must:

- ▶ know everything about the destination and the road to that destination.
- ▶ have been down the road many times before.
- ▶ have finished the journey with an understanding of how to do it better the next time.
- ▶ have taken copious notes during each journey, for the express purpose of preparing yourself to lead others down that road.

Do those things and the results will take care of themselves. But as you do, keep in mind what Coach said about direction and ego: Be less interested in having your own way and more in finding the best way.

Study Human Nature

During the journey, you should take the time to learn as much as you can about each of your "players" in order to help the team be the best it can be." Not just what they do best and what problems they are most capable of solving but who they are as people—what's going on in their lives (good and bad) that could be impacting their attitudes and performance. Coaches exhibiting this fundamental will:

- ▶ study human nature by reading, scrutinizing, questioning, and searching for answers.
- ▶ learn how to motivate all types of individuals and still build a strong unit.
- ▶ be flexible, knowing every player/employee presents a unique problem. (No two are alike, but patterns will emerge.)
- ▶ do everything possible to save a player, rather than taking the easy way out and sacrificing that player to prove a point.
- ▶ bind the unique talent, value, excellence, and opportunity for contribution to the team in every person you coach.

Are you looking at your team members on an individual basis and what makes them feel good and important to the organization? Are you treating people the way you would want to be treated when they succeed and fail? You can't study human nature if you don't take the time to know the humans you're working with every day.

Take Responsibility

You are not perfect and never will be. You will make mistakes. Own them and move on. You don't know everything, don't pretend to. You must realize, welcome, and assume responsibility for the team and strive to make the efforts of yourself and your followers contribute to the enrichment of personality, the achievement of more abundant living for others, and the improvement of all. Remember the second set of three rules Coach's father instilled in him when dealing with adversity and difficult situations: Don't whine, don't complain, and don't make excuses. The first time your team falls short, take responsibility for failing to set the right expectation. ("My fault, bad pass.") Then lead everyone, including yourself, to get better.

Practice Love and Balance

Your interests will be served as you serve others. You must see how close to perfection you can get regarding your love for your team. Everything you do must be for them and not for yourself. That is balance. Perfect balance is the exact tension of multiple opposing forces. It requires keeping all things in the proper perspective. Exercise internal balance in your mind, body, and soul. Exercise external balance in your relationships, career, and finances. Seek consistency and avoid imbalanced reactions to life's peaks and valleys. And always maintain self-control and exercise patience in your leadership.

Coach practiced these fundamentals like he lived his entire life: always with consideration of others. Love was not a weakness to Coach but a leader's greatest strength. A true servant-leader, he knew how to respond in any situation and see the possibilities for individual growth through the close relationships and friendships he developed with everyone he served as a leader and coach.

As a coach, you must realize that you, above all else, are a servant and in a position of service. You serve your team, your team serves your customers and clients, and your customers and clients serve your greater purpose. Coach Wooden modeled the thinking, values, and behavior of a servant-leader—a person of nearly perfect love and balance. How important is love and balance in your life?

THE WOODEN WAY WORKsheet

A Teachable Point of View/A Position of SERVICE

What actions and behaviors describe how you serve? Using the word "service," build an acrostic that captures you/your organization's teachable point of view on what it means to be of SERVICE to others and what each word means for you. For example, "S" could stand for "**S**acrifice," an eagerness to make sacrifices for others.

S _____

E _____

R _____

V _____

I _____

C _____

E _____

"To whom much
is given,
much is required."

CHAPTER 11

Lesson Five:
How You Mentor

Lynn was getting ready to fly south and lead Victor Baez and his 20 coaches at Kansas City Royals' Dominican Republic Baseball Academy through the Coaching Success Course Series when Jeff Diskin, the Royals' director of professional development, "called an audible"—and changed the direction. Jeff, in talking with Victor, had realized the Royals needed to do something more than just work through the content. The academy, established in 1986, had grown dramatically in its 30-plus years. By outward appearances, it was thriving. But as Jeff explained to Lynn, the coaches didn't have a sense of unity in their approach to player development. In addition, their relationships weren't as good as he thought they could and should be with each other and the players. Jeff and Victor wanted a way to come together as a group around a new way of thinking—a new coaching and leadership philosophy.

Lynn knew what to do. He turned to The Pyramid of Success and devised an approach similar to what he had done with Jason and his team when he helped them create their six core values.

First, he helped Victor and the coaches understand what The Pyramid of Success's blocks of behavior were all about—how and why they were relevant for helping them become better coaches and what roles they could play in helping the island's best young baseball talent become successful in baseball and in life. Then he helped them define the parameters of the culture they wanted at the academy for developing those players as better athletes, students, and people—and for developing themselves as more effective coaches who could perhaps one day manage teams and, more important, their relationships with each other and in their lives in the future. After a week of work, they ended up with "One Royal Way: The Coaches Creed" (see Figure 11–1 on page 179), a statement of values, purpose, and cultural intention (which also happens to start with the Kansas City address of the Kansas City Royals). The Coaches' Creed consists of four pillars of behavior and performance built around effort, knowledge, love, and faith:

- *Effort.* As a life coach, enthusiastically invest your best effort every day, inspiring players to enthusiastically give their best effort. Recognize and embrace the opportunity, privilege, and responsibility to develop players and yourself to your highest levels of capability.
- *Knowledge.* As coaches, teachers, and lifelong learners, acquire and use a complete base of knowledge of players, the game, and the profession.
- *Love.* Do everything with love that always protects, trusts, hopes, perseveres, and never fails.
- *Faith.* As people of faith in God, yourself, and each other, as well as your preparation and abilities, embrace One Royal Way as the path to making extraordinary things happen. Believe that extraordinary performance occurs, as it should, provided you all do what you must as coaches pursuing perfection.

Like Jason's work with Lynn at GoldenComm, One Royal Way used the Pyramid as an inspiration and foundation for its own behaviors and values. It is as good an example as any of how an organization can shape the process of coaching and leading with the Pyramid. It also connects to the four previous lessons. With Victor guiding the other coaches, One

FIGURE 11–1 *One Royal Way's Application of The Pyramid of Success*

Royal Way delivers a philosophy that will shape the coaches' thinking and the quality of that thinking moving forward. It defines the behaviors they need to set the example for each other and the players. It focuses their teaching and provides the measure of the quality of their leadership.

The realization that the academy needed One Royal Way, however, started by seeing a deficiency in something paramount to the way Coach lived his life: the quality of your relationships. Coach believed that the level of his success and happiness in life was directly proportional to the quality of his relationships—the role models who inspired him, the partners who assisted him, the friends who supported him, and the mentors who guided him. These were the people who defined his life, shaped his growth, reinforced what he valued, and fulfilled him.

Lesson Five: How You Mentor—*harness the power in mentoring to improve yourself and to serve those you have the privilege to help develop—*speaks directly to the fourth relationship on Coach's list: the mentors. How have you been mentored? How are you being mentored and mentoring the leaders in your organization to become coaches and players to come together as a team? To coach yourself and your team way up for the long term, you must reflect on who your mentors are and have been, and how they have and continue to influence your thinking. Then you must consider your ability and eagerness to mentor others and be a "difference maker" in their lives.

YOUR MENTORS

To understand how to mentor, you must consider how you have been mentored, but what does that mean? How would you define "mentor"? It's one of those words often used but seldom understood and thought about on the level Coach that did. Ever the teacher, he liked to point out that the word "mentor" is both a noun and a verb: something you are and something you should do—and something over which you have much control. You choose who to sit with and who to ask to share your wisdom, experiences, and encouragement from a distance or close up, purposefully or by chance. Coach, the teacher, also knew the origin of the word "mentor": Homer's *Odyssey,* which he had studied, memorized, and taught. Before the Trojan War, Odysseus asks his friend Mentor to look after his family and home. When Odysseus needs help after returning from the war, the goddess Athena comes to his rescue in the form of his old friend Mentor.

Coach worked very hard to fill the role of Mentor—to develop, grow, strengthen, and function effectively in his relationships as a supportive friend, a helpful partner, an inspirational model of behavior, and a mentor providing guidance. Mentoring was something Coach felt he needed to have and do—he needed to be a mentor and to have mentors in all parts of his life: personal, professional, spiritual, and in leadership. In each of those areas, Coach found people indirectly and directly to learn from. Some were deeply personal relationships; some he never could know personally but were a result of his relentless search for learning, guidance, and wisdom.

Consider the relationships you have and the ones that are influencing you the most (or could influence you more) as you read how Coach thought of his mentors. Do you have someone who has provided mentoring in your life in each of those four areas? Where are you finding mentoring, and where are you falling short and need to find mentoring?

Personal Mentors

Coach's father, Joshua, was, without question, the most important personal (and overall) mentor in his life, and he demonstrated what it meant to be a good person no matter the circumstance. From the two sets of three rules he had for all his children to the Seven Point Creed he gave Coach when he graduated grade school, Joshua was Coach's greatest living example of love (especially in how he treated Coach's mother), gentleness (despite great physical strength), equality (treating all people with dignity and respect), and humility (always be the best you can be and help others who are no better than anyone else because you're no better than anyone else).

Personal mentors teach you about things like humility, contentment, and living well with family and friends. They encourage, challenge, and provide correction and redirection to keep you focusing on the right things in the right ways. They help you keep your priorities straight and remind you not to compromise on what matters most to you, because their principles and values direct(ed) their behavior and actions as they live(d) their lives.

Professional Mentors

Coach's three basketball coaches taught him great lessons in leadership, but he considered them professional mentors, none more than Ward "Piggy" Lambert, his coach at Purdue University. Coach described Piggy as someone who "never seemed to see limitations—only possibilities"— who let experience be the teacher, and who taught and demonstrated to Coach that it was often necessary to tell the team and individuals what they needed to hear, rather than what they wanted to hear. Piggy provided the example and lessons that shaped the philosophy, demeanor, team principles, decision-making, and personal principles that guided Coach's career and professional success.

Professional mentors set an example and offer counsel that inspires, directs, develops, and shapes your goals and aspirations in your chosen vocation. They can help with philosophy, process, practices, strategy, problem solving, and effective work habit development. They can also be catalysts that help you take risks and seize opportunities.

Spiritual Mentors

Coach wrote and spoke often of how he felt Mother Teresa was the greatest example of love, faith, devotion, and spiritual strength that he had studied and learned from in his journey of faith and life. It was her shining beacon of humility, grace, dedication, and unrelenting service to the lost and least of India's population that captured his heart and mind. It was his own questions of faith and the desire to serve and counsel his players on these same matters that took Coach to his knees in prayer and to study everything that was written by Mother Teresa and about her life and service.

Spiritual mentors give you faith, touch your soul, and teach you the importance of loving others. You don't need to follow any particular religion, or any religion, to need these things. You don't even need someone in person. Coach was constantly reading, learning, and reaching out to find understanding and answers to life's most profound questions. He found deep meaning, constant encouragement, and daily direction reading the Bible every day of his life—a healthy habit he learned from his father. Coach believed that God brings people into our lives at just the time we need guidance. To satisfy the deepest longings of his heart and soul and to know the God he believed gave him and his family life, he turned to men and women of faith and purpose within and beyond houses of worship. These "saints" provided an example, a great sense of purpose and meaning, hope in the darkest of days, and direction for every day.

Leadership Mentors

Coach's coaches certainly mentored him as a leader, but for all the leaders Coach learned from in person, he genuinely felt he had been mentored by Abraham Lincoln. He found lessons on integrity, wisdom, and strength in Lincoln's writings and biographies about the 16th president of the United States. Coach admired the deep sense of responsibility Lincoln felt in his life and presidency, and the way in which he wrestled and handled the crushing weight of moral agony. Coach also felt Lincoln "taught" him valuable lessons on failure (how and why it happens, how to respond to it, and how to learn and grow from these experiences). He even memorized extensive passages of Lincoln's speeches that he could use as a leader in his own life.

Leadership mentors guide you through the many roles you will play in your life: teammate, captain, soldier, lieutenant, partner/husband/wife, mother/father, assistant coach, and head coach. You need renewed and different strength and purpose in each of these roles, so you must continue to learn from all those who serve(d), thrive(d), and were or are in positions of leadership. Quiet strength, strong conviction, measured deliberate actions, humility, courage, tireless effort, and dedication to cause and serving others . . . these were the things Coach admired in the leaders he followed and learned to provide as he led and mentored others every day of his life, long after he retired from coaching the game of basketball. (He never retired from coaching the game of life.)

THE WOODEN WAY WORKsheet

Your Mentors

Consider the four types of mentors that impacted Coach Wooden's life. Can you identify at least one mentor you had or have in these areas and the most important mentoring lesson (something that you found vital in your life) from each?

Personal Mentor and the lesson that person taught me.

_____

_____

_____

Professional Mentor and the lesson that person taught me.

_____

_____

_____

THE WOODEN WAY WORKsheet

Spiritual Mentor and the lesson that person taught me.

_____

_____

_____

Leadership Mentor and the lesson that person taught me.

_____

_____

_____

Now, ask yourself: Are there any areas of your life where wise counsel and a good example could help you improve your perspective, decisions, and actions? Who might be able to provide mentoring for you in those areas? What are your plans to reach out to this person?

_____

_____

_____

_____

_____

_____

_____

YOUR MENTORING

It was a dark, cold, and snowy February night in 2004 when Lynn joined Coach at the United States Air Force Academy. Now 93 years old, Coach had been invited to be a guest speaker at the Academy's National Character & Leadership Symposium. This was the kind of night a 93-year-old man absolutely shouldn't be out in, but it could have been 50 below and Coach wouldn't have cancelled. A former lieutenant in the Navy, he felt a sense of duty to the cadets he would be speaking to and wouldn't miss the opportunity to talk to some of America's best and brightest young men and women.

Coach arrived a little less than an hour before the program was supposed to start. The cadets were already gathered in the auditorium when he came in from the cold through the doors at the back. Hand on his cane, a long overcoat enveloping his 145-pound frame, Coach's body hardly struck an imposing figure physically. But at the sight of his face, the respect those cadets showed for him is something Lynn will never forget. As he came into view, one cadet yelled, "There he is!" and simultaneously the 4,200 cadets in attendance stood, turned, and applauded.

Coach gave his standard 45-minute talk that night, took questions, and then he returned the cadets' respect by sitting at a table to greet and sign programs, Pyramids, books, and photos or just to meet anyone who wanted to meet him. He stayed for two hours. Lynn asked several times if he wanted to leave, but there was no moving him. Coach had been touched by the opportunity to speak to and meet the cadets that night and share some of his wisdom. He commented on what great shape he felt the country was in based on all the young leaders before him. He believed connecting with those young men and women and providing some level of mentoring with his words wasn't just an opportunity but his responsibility to the potential and power of mentoring others.

Mentoring others is about recognizing where you are in your life and what you have the opportunity and responsibility to share—and it should excite you! To understand the power of mentoring is to recognize how far you have come and how much you have to offer—that you can see and can help someone in a personal, professional, spiritual, or leadership capacity or at least have the ability to see when mentoring is needed. That's certainly what Jeff Diskin saw was needed in the Royals' baseball academy and Jason needed at GoldenComm. So, they brought in Lynn to mentor them on The Pyramid of Success and guide them to their new core values.

What Lynn also showed them is how connected mentoring is to improving both the quality of your relationships *and* the quality of your thinking. It is the transformational step in coaching them and you way up and leading the Wooden Way—to becoming what he calls a "difference maker" (see Figure 11–2 on page 187) in others' lives.

The Difference Maker diagram is a model for the lessons you have learned in this part of the book, but unlike The Pyramid of Success, it builds from the top down, continually establishing a new foundation until you reach the point of mentorship and seeing your own progress. Your first time through, you become a difference maker for yourself, finding your own mentors to coach you way up. Then, you start over again. The need for continual coaching forces you back through the lessons to reconsider the quality of your thinking when it comes to others, how you set the example, how you lead, how you teach, and how you mentor—and then do it again and again and again . . .

Just like Coach, every "season" you repeat the lessons. The mentoring that comes into your life is going to compel you to improve in every area, especially the quality of thinking as you mentor. Coach wanted his mentoring to cause people to think. He believed that it was much more important to get his assistants and players to improve the quality of their thinking (and thus their character) than it was to tell them what to think. He knew when everyone is thinking the same, nobody is thinking. That's why he was reluctant to give advice and would only share his opinion when asked. That was true for the game of basketball and even truer for the game of life. He did not need to be the smartest person in the room but found it helpful to have smart people around him whose thinking he would constantly seek and apply. That included his players whose ideas he often implemented in key situations, bringing them along through the lessons, making them the examples: the teachers, leaders, and mentors.

That's what Coach did for Lynn, Diane Rentfrow first did and now a Vistage group does for Jason, and Lynn does for GoldenComm and the Royals: As mentors, they first and foremost challenged the quality of the

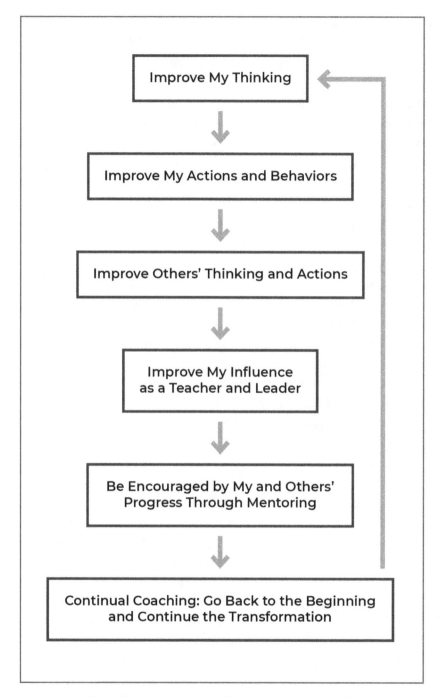

FIGURE 11-2 *The Difference Maker: Traditional Coaching the "Wooden Way"*

thinking being done. For Lynn, too many coaches and leaders are like the old "Quick Draw McGraw" cartoon where he says: "I'll do the thinking around here." That may make you feel good and comfortable. But it isn't going to coach you or the team way up. "There is something in everyone that fundamentally feeds what makes you feel the best and appear to be your best. That place in which you really enjoy what you do and how you're feeling about it," says Lynn. "And you're never lost trying to find that pleasurable place. You look for the circumstances in which you feel your best. Mentoring can be that, but that also means being able to let go and create new leaders in the organization."

Letting go is what all leaders struggle with at some point. As their businesses grow, they get pulled in different directions, and they take on new responsibilities that push them out of their comfort zone. Jason is confronting this need to let go as he reassesses himself, keeps getting back on the Pyramid, and continually strives to be a difference maker. Because he knows without it the team and his business will not keep growing.

"I love doing the work," Jason says. "I can't stop doing it. It's fun, and that's a big problem. That's why a lot of athletes don't make great coaches. They never stop working and want to keep playing. I have to understand that I can't expect everyone to work like me when I was in my 20s. Never going home. Never leaving work unfinished even if it wasn't due yet. I give people work to do on Friday, and they say they will get to it on Monday. I would have never said that to my boss when I was their age. But that isn't what everybody does. And when I get work that is good but not exactly as good as I want it, I have a tendency to take it back and do it myself. 'Good job, good effort, you're off the project, I'm taking over, and we'll go over later why it didn't work.' I'll do that to my number two guy! That's my expectation of performance, and we have a relationship that can take it. But I realize there is something in that expectation of performance that is dark and keeping me from being the mentor and coach I want to be."

What it comes down to for Jason and most leaders is what Lynn said: safety and comfort. We all need to work on getting uncomfortable and being vulnerable enough to admit where you are failing yourself and others. Coach never stopped working on being better, being his best, or being productive, even after he started winning championships. "Being satisfied is always your enemy," Coach would often say, even after he retired. He wanted himself, his team, his system, and everyone he served to get better. That had as much to do with improving his thinking about others as it did with the team's skills.

Of course, in many ways, Jason was already doing this type of mentoring and practicing the lessons of the Wooden Way. That's why he was able to build a successful company and be open to changing the core values and the platforms on which the company operated. "I was already thinking about the thinking before I met Lynn," Jason says. "I always look into projects and ask 'Who is doing the thinking?' Two years after meeting Lynn, my people know we are going to talk about the quality of our thinking every day. It has morphed into a powerful culture change for us. Conversations are happening with me, and even better, when I'm not in the room, which is making for better relationships. The employees love each other. That can happen in organizations. But I can't rest on that. I'm aware more than ever of how I set the example as I guide my leadership team. While we have unmetered vacation and sick days, I always ask permission from the leadership team to take vacation and send them pictures when I'm away thanking them for making it possible. I also make sure they know I am there to help. I'll walk around and ask, 'Is there anything I can do for you?' If the answer is 'no,' I tell them to think hard because 'I have an innate need to be needed. It hurts my feelings if no one needs me.'"

Jason sees feedback as essential in satisfying this need and guiding himself and others: "At GoldenComm all team members are encouraged to accept and give feedback that improves self and team. We see this in our day-to-day activities, our peer reviews, and our quarterly recaps. Feedback reduces uncertainty, solves problems, builds trust, improves work quality, compels transparency, and strengthens relationships. But here's the catch, and Lynn showed me it goes back to the Pyramid: Feedback needs to be presented with the right intentness. Coach knew the best way to improve the team is to improve yourself first. When giving or receiving feedback, remember that the information presented is for the encouragement and betterment of the team *and* yourself. Whatever feedback you receive, know it's a gift to improve yourself."

Not that the feedback is easy to take, as Jason learned when he and his team took Lynn's assessments. He thought he was doing better than he was, especially when it came to the relationships at the company. In fact, Jason learned through feedback from Lynn and his team that his need to be needed and mentor *outside* the company was affecting his work inside the company, as well as his ability to make it home on time. He was spending 25 hours a week at a high school mentoring the football coach and the principal, and it consumed his thinking. "If you would give us the attention you would give the people you are mentoring outside the company," one of his leaders said. "If you want this company to grow like I know you want it to grow, you better start giving it the same attention you're giving the high school."

It is easy to get distracted and not find the balance you need with your people. But if you come from a place of love, you can build the relationships and the quality of them. You can be that difference maker. Bill Walton, perhaps Coach's most politically active and controversial athlete, told a story to Lynn when they shared the stage at a gathering of financial industry executives in Newport Beach, California: He had traveled with Coach to Washington, DC, after Coach retired to give a speech. They decided to stop and visit the Vietnam and Lincoln Memorials. At the Vietnam Memorial, they prayed together for friends and classmates who had lost their lives. At the Lincoln Memorial, Coach perfectly recited the Gettysburg Address as tears streamed down the faces of both men. Coach was still teaching and mentoring, and Walton was still learning. As are we all, if we keep working on it.

THERE FOR OTHERS, ALWAYS

It was early March 2005 and Lynn was meeting with Coach at his condo in Encino, California. In the conversation, Lynn shared with Coach a story of his Shelby High School Class of 1964 basketball teammate, Steve Smith. "Smitty," or "Cue Ball" (he had shaved his head in high school—long before it became a "thing"), had gone on to become an Ohio High School Hall of Fame coach at Orrville, Ohio. (Home to another Hall of Fame coach, Indiana's Bobby Knight—the gym in Orrville is named after Knight, the court is named for Smith.) Lynn told Coach that Smith was in the late stages of brain cancer.

Lynn told Coach that Steve had always wanted to meet him. He had been a student of Coach Wooden's teachings, especially when it came to the importance of effort and the fundamentals. But he had not been able to make the trip from Ohio to California, and now he was entering his final days. Lynn asked Coach if they could give Steve a call. He wasn't sure the call would go well, but it was worth a try. Coach said he would be happy to.

Steve's wife, Donna, who Lynn had known since high school, answered the phone and said to her husband, "Coach Wooden is on the line and wants to talk to Coach Smith." What happened next Donna called a miracle: For 20 minutes Steve was at the top of his game mentally and had an energetic, inspired conversation on life, basketball, coaching, and family. Coach complimented Coach Smith on accomplishing something that he had wanted but never been able to do: Win a high school state championship. The two great coaches said their goodbyes. "See you soon, Coach," they said to each other.

Steve Smith passed away two weeks later. He was 59.

THE WOODEN WAY WORKsheet

Your Mentoring

Take stock of your current mentoring activity in your personal and professional life. Who are you serving as a mentor? On what areas of life is that mentoring focused?

THE WOODEN WAY WORKsheet

_____

_____

_____

How effective are you in that mentoring, and what is the possible impact you are having?

_____

_____

_____

Are there any areas of your life or someone who recently reached out to you for help where *your* wise counsel and good example could help others improve their perspective, decisions, and actions?

_____

_____

_____

_____

_____

_____

Answering the Call to Greatness and Goodness

Where is your call to coach and lead coming from?

I n leading and coaching the Wooden Way, you are either being called or being called out—or both. If you're screwing up, someone has already called you out on it—or will. . . . If you have already stepped up to coach, the Wooden Way is a wake-up call like it was for each one of us—to call *yourself* out and step up even more and make each day your masterpiece. Building a better you builds a better world as you develop more coaches and leaders who answer their own calls to greatness and goodness.

*"If we magnified blessings
as much as we magnify
disappointments, we would
all be much happier."*

CHAPTER 12

Your Masterpiece

O n June 4, 2020, the day before his son Cole's graduation from high school, Lynn wrote him a letter. Like almost all senior years across the county that spring, Cole's had not been what anyone wanted or expected. Sure, he would get an in-person graduation the next day, but due to the Covid-19 pandemic, it would be a socially distanced and masked affair. The last weeks in school and with the good friends he had made there were screen-to-screen not face-to-face. The prom and senior trip didn't happen. Worst of all, Cole's final baseball season, which started with dreams, anticipation, and hope of playing in college, had been cancelled ten games in.

Cole was heartbroken and rightfully so. It didn't seem fair—and it wasn't. But sometimes life isn't fair, and Lynn wanted his son to know that. While it was hard for Cole to see it at the time, getting through this difficult period would make him better prepared to handle what came next in his life. "God has made you to handle life challenges," Lynn wrote. "And be sure that you know, beyond a shadow of a doubt, that God has a special master plan and purpose for your life. Adversity always makes you stronger because it pulls out the strength that lies within you."

Cole knew all too well about adversity making him stronger. He had nearly died when he was eight from Stevens-Johnson syndrome, a rare and serious disorder of the skin and mucous membranes. Coach had been alive when Cole got sick. Coach had known Cole since the day he was born. A Pyramid of Success had hung on Cole's wall most of his life. Cole had heard his father share so much Wooden wisdom that Lynn wouldn't blame him for saying "enough already, Dad." Cole had even flown on a private jet to Lynn's alma mater, Western Michigan University, where Lynn interviewed Coach in front of 9,000 people, including some of Coach's former players. Cole helped Coach sign Pyramids for his audience that day, and he gave Cole the first dollar he ever earned.

When Cole had gotten sick, Coach was there. Lynn remembers the hug Coach gave him, his hand on Lynn's shoulder, his words softly and lovingly spoken, "faith and patience."

Lynn wanted Cole to always know how lucky he and his wife are and would be to have Cole as their son, thanking him for the amazing experience they had watching him grow as a student, an athlete, and a fine young man. He made sure that Cole knew how important loyalty would be for him and his family in the future. Coach taught that everyone has to be loyal to someone and something if you are to have the self-respect you need to become the best person you are meant to be. Dream big, Lynn told Cole: "All the things you have seen on The Pyramid of Success will help you be your best."

Those words held extra significance for Lynn as he finished the letter that evening. June 4, 2020 was the tenth anniversary of Coach's passing. Those words were also significant, because earlier that spring, Lynn had failed them with Cole.

FALLING OFF THE PYRAMID: LYNN'S STORY, PART II

Cole was feeling the pressure to announce where he was going to attend college and have, "you know, Dad, that college experience," but he had been reeling the last couple of months. Covid-19 had shut down all the things that were supposed to be the highlights of his senior year and put in jeopardy his opportunity to play college ball and perhaps beyond—to chase the Big Dream, which began when he was about six.

I had been the self-appointed agent and recruiting coach. For 18 months I had logged hundreds of hours researching schools and conferences, reviewing rosters and bios of coaches, and filling out athletic program questionnaires. Letters of introduction and accomplishment were complete. Highlight videos shot and sent. Target schools identified. Correspondence managed. This was all work that seemed necessary, and I was enjoying the process, as well as the sense of possibilities. We had received more than just encouraging feedback from coaches to fuel my excitement and energy. Not from the NCAA Division 1 where Cole, they said, needed another five miles per hour on his fastball. But Division II and III, NAIA, and junior college programs, a few of which had made offers that were attractive. I had covered all the bases, done all the "necessary" things for Cole. After all, this was his Big Dream.

Or so I thought. I had missed something. Something important. I had forgotten some important wisdom from Coach: The worst things you can do for your children are the things they could and should do for themselves. Much of what I dove into are things Cole should have taken the initiative to do. But I had charged ahead and missed important signals on what it was he wanted and needed. Cole had talked plenty about the "want to" play baseball, but over his senior year he seemed less engaged and interested in the "have to." When baseball was shut down by the pandemic so was Cole's energy, enthusiasm, and sense of optimism about our future in baseball . . . his future. He was not sure that he wanted to give all the effort, dedication, and commitment that a college baseball program would expect. He was now reluctant to consider a college that was far from home and liked more and more the choice his friends were making: Grand Canyon University in Phoenix, Arizona; it had the sports and business management curriculum he was interested in pursuing. As for baseball? He said he could find somewhere to play "for fun."

I tried not to show my emotions, but I was furious, disappointed, and heartbroken. All that eventually came out in a heated out-of-control conversation with Cole that made nothing better and left me ashamed of how I acted and reacted. I had failed to walk the talk of the Wooden Way and stay on The Pyramid of Success. In my exuberance to "make things happen," I failed to consider others. I was taking care of everything but listening to my son and what he wanted. I had forgotten 20 years of study with Coach and The Pyramid of Success—all the mentoring and practice of the principles that I knew had prepared me for this opportunity to be a good parent, teacher, and coach for my son.

First and foremost, I lacked self-control by letting my emotions get the best of me. But it was my foundational failure when it came to the Pyramid that hurt the most. Of course, I had shown plenty of industriousness and enthusiasm for the work and helping Cole realize his dream. But I explained away Cole's fading industriousness and enthusiasm as a symptom of the pandemic. As for foundation blocks of friendship and cooperation? Friendship comes from mutual respect and devotion; I held Cole's baseball talents in high regard but neglected to give him respect for his growing devotion and desire to define and have the college experience he wanted. And cooperation? Cole's words will hopefully ring in my ears for all my days if and when I fall off the Pyramid again: "Dad, you are not listening to me. That is not what I want to do or where I want to go to school."

Bad teacher, bad coach, bad parent.

Building stronger relationships with those you love is what keeps you on track to be the person you are meant to be. I knew I couldn't undo any of what happened, but I knew how to move forward. I apologized for being a jerk and asked for and received forgiveness from my wife, Tracy, and Cole, who will attend the school of his choice.

As for baseball? Cole will find a way to play for fun. He has new dreams to pursue. It's his masterpiece to make now.

"MAKE EACH DAY YOUR MASTERPIECE"

Those words were the third point in the Seven Point Creed Joshua Wooden gave Coach. Only "be true to yourself" and "help others" came before it on the list—and rightly so. Joshua knew you can't make any day a masterpiece if you're inauthentic and serving only yourself, which was a big reason Lynn initially failed Cole. What did Joshua mean by "make each day your masterpiece"? It meant what Lynn realized when he turned around his mistake: Yesterday is finished and cannot be changed. A better tomorrow can only be a result of what you do today.

For Coach, true success only came from the satisfaction one gets from knowing you did the best you can do. Doing your best today and every day moving forward was his key to that better tomorrow. Coach often counseled a player who was not giving their best on a particular day with these words: "Don't think you can make up for it by working twice as hard tomorrow. If you have it within your power to work twice as hard, why aren't you doing it now? If you don't have the time to do it right, where will you find the time to do it over?" Maximum effort and preparation always pay dividends in improved performance and produce the best work your talent, experience, energy, and commitment can bring forth.

Making each day your masterpiece does not mean your whole masterpiece is created in a day. Each day is the chance for one masterful brush stroke. Every task you complete is an opportunity to undo a mistake or do something better and increase your chances of doing it even better the next time.

And when you're putting forth that effort, do what Lynn did in his letter and recall the final point on Joshua Wooden's Seven Point Creed: Pray for guidance and count and give thanks for your blessings every day. Too often we take our blessings for granted. We fail to give thanks because we are busy looking at what we don't have versus what we do have. We tend to think we can do it all ourselves and fail to ask for guidance and assistance—from anyone be that God, a mentor, a friend. . . . When we look at our blessings—family, friends, good health, and the beauty around us—we see those things that truly matter.

Once we are used to giving thanks, it's easier to ask for guidance and assistance. Asking for help isn't a sign of weakness in a coach and leader; it's an everyday process of recognizing where the real blessings in life come from that give us strength. Without that strength, you'll never answer Coach's call to greatness and goodness.

THE WOODEN WAY WORKsheet

Making Each Day Your Masterpiece

Can you recall a day that you would describe as a masterpiece day? What transpired on that day that made it a masterpiece?

_____

_____

_____

_____

What keeps you from having more of these "masterpiece days"?

_____

_____

_____

_____

Our country has a national holiday in which we give thanks and remind ourselves to do it more and more. But why do we need to wait for one day? Think about a daily moment of thinking and action in which you create a "Thanksgiving Moment." Start with yourself. What are you thankful for? Your physical and mental health? Family? Friends? Are you taking any of these things for granted?

_____

_____

_____

_____

THE WOODEN WAY WORKsheet

How do you react and feel when someone thanks you or is thankful for you?

_____

_____

_____

_____

Coach tried every day to perform a kindness task: He did something every day that would benefit others with no thought of anything in return. Are you a helper or someone who always needs to be helped? Can you recall the acts of kindness you performed in the last week? Make a list of acts of kindness you can perform in the next week.

_____

_____

_____

_____

ANSWERING THE CALL TO GREATNESS AND GOODNESS

Early in this book, we said if Jim Collins showed us how to go from good to great, John Wooden showed us how to go from goodness to greatness—to care for others and build character and values that lead to outstanding performance. This is true but, we confess, not quite right. While goodness to greatness is a nice parallel to Collins' words, Dick Enberg got it right in his eulogy: Coach's greatness was _exceeded_ by his goodness: _Coach didn't_ *show us how to go from goodness to greatness. He showed us how to go from greatness to goodness.*

Coach showed how to get the competitive greatness out of a team by getting that greatness out of yourself first: to "be at your best when your best is needed"—to achieve his definition of success and have the peace of mind and self-satisfaction that come from making the effort to become the best of which you are capable of becoming. The Wooden Way can take you and your team to that place of extraordinary performance but not without the care and consideration of yourself and others. But you can't be right as a leader of your people if you are not right with yourself first. Every leader says they want to make their companies more meaningful and purposeful. That meaning and purpose can only start with the dedication and inspiration of the leader to coach from a place of love. You can't reach, teach, and serve your people if you don't love them, and you can't love them if you don't have love in your heart for yourself.

That is your legacy. It's as simple as that. There is no wizardry in these pages, just a practical and pragmatic guide for continuous improvement backed by the deep wisdom of Coach Wooden. Like he said, there are no tricks in the game (at least not for long). Just love and balance in all things and that care and consideration for others to build better relationships. And that work starts with you before it starts with them.

Coach was asked after each championship season if the team cutting down the nets was the greatest he'd ever coached. Coach would respond by paraphrasing the words of another legendary coach, Amos Alonzo Stagg, "I won't know that for another 20 years." He had no idea what his players would become. Greatness and goodness were not about what they achieved on the scoreboard but the people they were going to be and the impact they would have on the world in which we live. He believed in their character. He hoped there would be great teachers and leaders, husbands, and fathers. But he could only coach them up way up for so long. After that, it was up to them to continue the path and hear the call to greatness and goodness. *Do you hear this call?*

We hope you do. But remember the need for alertness: Once you hear that call, it keeps coming—and you need to answer it. It's what we strive to do every day, and no, not every day is a masterpiece. Far from it. We're still getting called out and working on it in our homes and lives—even as we were writing this book. Jason realized how far he has to go in mentoring his team and how he has fallen short in keeping his promise to be home when he said he would. Being a father and there for his son every day for 18 years wasn't something that Lynn ever took for granted, given that Guerin men had been walking away from their boys for over a hundred years, and yet he fell off the Pyramid right when his son needed him most. But we've been fortunate enough to be given a foundation from Coach to have the courage to admit our mistakes and shortcomings and take action to work on them. If we allow the fear of failure or hard work to keep us from acting, we will never achieve Coach's definition of success or reach our full potential. Let's face it: We're all imperfect, and we're going to fall short on occasion. As Coach reminded himself almost daily, "I'm not the person I want to be. I'm not the person I'm going to be. But I'm glad that I'm better than the person I used to be." Coach called life a four-quarter game. No matter what quarter you are in, you can still finish strong like Coach did by taking the initiative to answer the call to greatness and goodness. That's how the journey goes as we become coaches the Wooden Way.

So, coach, as you go back through this book and keep working on it, we have one last request: Take 20 seconds every morning before you start your day, stand in front of the mirror, and say "I'm a coach. I have the opportunity to be my best and help and serve and coach others to be their best, and I'm going to coach myself and them way up today." Then walk out the door. Let those words be your mantra and Coach's lessons and his Pyramid of Success be your guides. It's time to answer the call. Use all you've learned as you take on each day the Wooden Way with every person you have the privilege to teach, coach, and serve. You have been given a gift of wisdom, peace of mind, and perspective to share with others.

Giving this gift each day will make every day a masterpiece.

Acknowledgments

FROM LYNN

Being involved in the development and writing of this book has been a pure Coach Wooden experience. With him, the experience was always about learning and teaching, and I have learned so much in working on this book. Hopefully, we have helped develop something that can teach others, so they can learn and teach others.

Coach modeled the family first, and so will I in my gratitude. To my wonderful wife Tracy, my two sons, Kyle and Cole, my daughter-in-law Melissa, and my grandsons, Wade and Trey: You are the most important people in my life. You make every day rich and full of purpose and meaning. You are why dad and grandpa must keep "working on it."

To my partner Jason Lavin and our writer Jim Eber: You're great teammates. You played this game so well and you're committed to keep working on it and playing the game of life best you can. You made everyone on the book team better.

To my Wooden "teammate" Craig Impelman, you're an amazing coach and student of all things Coach. No one has more

Wooden Wisdom. You make the world a better place with your passion to coach and your amazing positive attitude.

To the Wooden Family: thank you for the opportunity to carry on the rich tradition of teaching and coaching the Wooden Way.

To my mother Evelyn Guerin, my first and most loyal and loving coach: You gave up everything for your boys. There was nothing more you could have done or better example you could have set. And to my brother Tom Guerin: Your steadfast love and balance was so important in my life. You're my teammate for life and eternity.

To my spiritual mentor pastor Pete Mckenzie. For the past 26 years, you have taught, coached, and modeled what it means to be a "man of God—absolutely." I and thousands of other men are eternally grateful.

Finally, to my earliest coaching mentors: Ohio's Shelby High School Whippets Coaching Hall of Famers, Ron Strine, Bill Wilkins, and Bill Varble. You prepared me to work with the greatest coach ever. I could understand Coach's greatness and goodness because I had seen much of it modeled by the men you were. Men of values, principles, high morals, uncompromising integrity, and character. You always gave your best and challenged and taught me how to give my best.

FROM JASON

A village of people deserve my gratitude for bringing this book to life, but a few deserve to be called out by name, starting with my teammates at GoldenComm who make the place happen, especially the leadership team (Andrew, Mic, Audra, Jessica, Brian, and Peggy). I "left my post" several times the last couple years to work on this book, and none of you missed a play, pandemic and all. You guys compete at the highest level every day, and I am lucky to be surrounded by you.

To the neighborhood kids and parents of Newport Beach who allowed me to coach baseball, football, and soccer throughout the decades: Those years have been the best thousands of hours I could ask for. And of course, the cul-de-sac of "Grove Lane," the McGees and the Olsons, who are like family. It's as if we had three homes on the block. Thank you for all your love and support.

Ryan Shea, CEO of Entrepreneur Media, thank you for being a person where a breakfast meeting and handshake is still a way to get business done. Your faith and patience in this book are the reasons *Coach' Em Way Up* made it to press. And to his team at Entrepreneur Press, led by Jen Dorsey, thank you for never giving up either.

And, of course, none of this happens without my co-authors Jim Eber and Lynn Guerin. I have only known you for a couple years, but I feel like I've known you both all of my life. Jim, you not only took what we had and made a wonderful story, but you made our program better. Lynn, you are so wise, like Coach Wooden—boy am I blessed to have run into you.

My mom and dad, Michelle and Dave, and my mother- and father-in-law, Marilynn and Jim: I speak for my whole family when I say thank you for the unconditional love and support. We're nowhere without the four of you coaching us up for the last 20-plus years in our marriage and 50-plus years in our lives.

Finally and most important to me: To Brenda, my wife and best friend, thank you for putting up with countless twists and turns as I added this book to my already crowded schedule; and to my three awesome kids, Cole, Sheya, and Jimmy: thank you for being my testing ground for many of The Pyramid of Success trials and errors. My highest honor is to be your dad. I love you more than words can say.

About the Authors

LYNN GUERIN is a highly accomplished executive, consultant, coach, keynote speaker, facilitator, and motivator with in-depth knowledge and skill in management and coaching, business communication, leadership development, and team development. He is the CEO of The John R. Wooden Course and the president and "Head Coach" of his family-owned coaching, training, and performance development firm, Guerin Marketing Services in Temecula, California. His mission is to make a powerful impact on the businesses he serves and the lives he touches and to help his clients and team become the best they are capable of becoming in the marketplace and in life.

Lynn has worked nationally and internationally with some of the world's most successful companies, including IBM, Toyota, Mercedes-Benz, Infiniti, Nissan, Acura, Hyundai Motor America, Kia, Chick-fil-A, In-N-Out, General Motors, Pacific Dental Services, Bernie Moreno Companies, Bobby Rahal Automotive, QK Healthcare Inc., Bazooka Brands, GoldenComm, and Nestlé

Purina. Today, The John R. Wooden Course is the centerpiece of Lynn's consulting and coaching practice, which helps organizations develop extraordinary teams and coaching culture and transforms managers into effective head coaches and leaders. His practice also includes a professional certification process to train and prepare professional coaching practitioners, educators, and executives to learn, teach, speak on, and apply Coach Wooden's principles including The Pyramid of Success.

Lynn received his B.A. in Liberal Arts and Business and his M.A. in International Studies from Western Michigan University. He lives in Temecula, California, with his wife, Tracy. He has two sons, Kyle (a service marketing director in the dental industry) and Cole (who studies sports management at Grand Canyon University), and two grandsons. His family attends Rancho Christian Church.

JASON LAVIN is a coach, speaker, and CEO with more than 25 years' experience enhancing the performance of individuals, teams, and organizations. He is the founder and CEO of Golden Communications, Inc. (GoldenComm), which has offices in Newport Beach (California), Salt Lake City (Utah), Wroclaw (Poland), and Pune (India). In 2017, GoldenComm hired Lynn Guerin for leadership and development training, and they became partners in The John R. Wooden Course.

As a coach, Jason has worked with youth sports teams to Fortune 100 companies. Leveraging The Pyramid of Success, he adapts his coaching process to the leaders he works with and the behaviors and cultures of their organizations to help them with their missions, visions, values, and whys. As an award-winning Vistage International Speaker, Jason has been teaching internet marketing seminars since 2009 and has spoken to thousands of CEOs and marketing executives. In 2015, he was named Vistage International's Fast Track Speaker of the Year, delivering more than 100 presentations in under three years while receiving near-perfect scores for those presentations.

Jason and his wife, Brenda, have three kids (Cole, Sheya, and Jimmy) and live in Newport Beach (and part time in Sandy, Utah). Jason and Brenda are active in their church and their kids' schools (Newport Harbor High School and Brighton High School in Cottonwood Heights, Utah).

He is also the president of the Newport Harbor High School Football Boosters (and is always fundraising for the school). He is a graduate of the University of Southern California.

Index

CPSIA information can be obtained
at www.ICGtesting.com
Printed in the USA
JSHW040907250920
8205JS00002B/7